VATICAN JOURNAL

1921–1954

Anne O'Hare McCormick

VATICAN JOURNAL

1921-1954

compiled and edited by

MARION TURNER SHEEHAN

with an introduction by

CLARE BOOTHE LUCE

NEW YORK

FARRAR, STRAUS AND CUDAHY

Contents

PART TWO : SPIRITUAL ESSAYS OF
HISTORICAL SIGNIFICANCE

INTRODUCTION

Of all the women I have ever known, Anne O'Hare McCormick was the most admirable. She was a wonderfully agreeable companion—gay, but never trivial, frank, but never tactless, inquisitive, but never obtrusive. She listened with sympathy to the opinions of others, and expressed her own with charity. Profoundly interested—as her profession demanded—in controversial subjects, her discussion of them was stimulating, and often provocative, but never contentious. The gentle modesty with which she put forth her own views, saved her converse, as it did her writing, from any appearance of that didacticism or prejudice which has so often destroyed the effectiveness of other speakers and writers. A compassionate and loving spirit, she "hated the sin, but loved the sinner."

When she was driven to censure by men or events, she avoided the note of rancor or bitterness. Accordingly, everyone who ever had the pleasure of spending any time with Anne, either as friend or colleague, left her presence a happier and a wiser person. But she took as fully as she gave: she brought out of others not only the "best" in them, but extracted from them every fact and piece of information that would serve her one abiding purpose: the enlightenment of her fellow countrymen about the great issues of the day— the issues that, rightly understood and courageously met, spelled peace and prosperity for them and their dear ones, but if ignored or misunderstood, could mean suffering and war.

In the secular, as well as in the religious sense, she had a catholic mind: she was interested in all the areas of knowledge which could have an impact on the well-being of the West.

The breadth of her information on the economic, cultural and political movements transpiring in our world was astonishing. Her interests ranged from ancient history to modern techniques in public housing construction, from the implication of nuclear fusion to the esthetic effect on New York's citizens of the gardens in Rockefeller Plaza. And she loved poetry too. There was poetry in Anne, as there was in her mother before her. In this collection of her columns, her references to Easter on Fifth Avenue are lyrical reporting. Delightfully, she never failed to mention the color, and variety, of the flowers on the women's hats in the Easter parade. Hers was a rare combination of a gentle and womanly spirit and a logical, unsentimental mind. Men, especially, never ceased to marvel that a woman so feminine had a mind so keen, so logical, and so well-stored with hard and uncontrovertible facts.

Anne's columns in the *New York Times* were read with eagerness and attention, not only by her "daily readers" but they were scanned even more eagerly by the journalists and statesmen of every other country in the world. Thinking people everywhere knew the profound influence her writing exercised on the opinions of millions of Americans. Over the years, her intuitiveness and the startling accuracy of many of her observations on current events and present rulers had made her "required reading" in foreign chancelleries, and in the editorial rooms of Europe's and Asia's most significant journals of opinion.

The columns in this book have been culled from her voluminous writings as examples of her extraordinary objectivity, even when reporting on the church of her own faith—the Roman Catholic Church. Her analyses here of its ancient laws, its organization, its influence on past and especially present history will appeal to all, whether Catholic or non-Catholic, who are interested in the role of religion in the world, and its close relation to the problem of finding viable solutions to the present struggle between the Communist and non-Communist world.

This is a book of historical scope.

It takes in the reign of Benedict XV, with Mrs. McCormick attending—in a frank mood—a session of the Papal Consistory at which he presided. Her analysis of the many-faceted personality of this Pontiff, and his effect upon the government of Italy, is both reporting of a high order, and excellent literature. Although Anne might have been a distinguished historian, she was serenely content to be a journalist, because she believed that in the modern world good journalism was its primary need.

After the death of this Pope, she saw and reported the "news behind the news" of the election of Pius XI. She describes and analyzes the troubled "Roman Question" which confronted the new Pontiff, and she carries us through the election of the present Pope, Pius XII, describing to us, with simplicity, candor and objectivity, the heartbreaking trials which confronted him, as he witnessed the fratricide between his Catholic children in World War II and the persecution of his flock in Communist lands.

Of especial interest is her illuminating chapter on Myron C. Taylor's appointment to the Vatican as the personal envoy of President Franklin D. Roosevelt. She explains why most of the non-Catholic countries of the world maintain diplomatic missions to the Holy See. She analyzes one of the most curious circumstances of our times—a circumstance incomprehensible to our allies and to all of the other world powers —that the United States, abjuring representation, finds itself in the company of the only two other major powers who do likewise: Red China and the Soviet Union.

Mrs. McCormick's description of the Roman Rota is of especial interest to those who are interested in the Church's views on annulment and divorce. She describes, in detail, the workings of the tribunal of the Rota. Members of the law profession, especially, will find a wealth of information about this ancient High Court of Christendom where "civil and ecclesiastical law has been a passion, a science and a fine art . . . a court of law with a long legal tradition and a history bound up with most of the great conflicts and events that have shaken civilization." Perhaps for the first time, the average reader will read a definite explanation of what constitutes an annulment and how the Church processes requests for them.

All of us who knew Anne as a friend are not surprised that her writings have often included thoughts that expressed her deep spirituality. And in this collection we come upon inspiring examples of it. A woman of pious wisdom as naturally as she breathed, Anne pled with her fellow creatures to recall the birth of the Christ-child and the redemptive sacrifice of the Christ-man. How could she fail to be concerned with the rising tide of irreligious forces which threaten to destroy the very fabric of our Western civilization? Her reflections at Eastertide and Christmastime, especially during the war years, challenge us all, as Christians or as men of good will. She calls upon men to unite—"one way or another the idea of unity, even the dream of peace, must come to pass if life on earth is to survive. With the spell of Bethlehem upon us, who can doubt the force of an idea or the final victory of faith?"

The last essay in the book, the very last time she put pen to paper before she died, reminds us that as long as there is the Easter renewal, whether in free countries or occupied countries, men can continue to hope if they will only look to the Light—the Light of the world which illuminates, and lifts up the hearts and souls of men and women who believe in God, and helps them to triumph over darkness, despair, and death. All those of us who must carry on in these hard days of uncertainty, confusion and conflict will find warmth in these reflections of the Light that burned so bright in the mind and heart of Anne O'Hare McCormick.

CLARE BOOTHE LUCE

Ridgefield, Connecticut
July 25, 1957

FOREWORD

Mrs. McCormick wrote exclusively for *The New York Times* from 1925 to 1954, with one exception when she consented to do some articles for the *Ladies Home Journal* in 1933-34. After graduating from St. Mary's College, Columbus, Ohio, Anne O'Hare married a young Dayton engineer and importer, Francis J. McCormick. It was during the early days of her travels abroad with her husband that she felt compelled to write about what she saw and especially about the people she met. She airmailed these dispatches to *The New York Times*. They were accepted, and from there on her readers began to look for Mrs. McCormick's column with mounting interest. Her Sunday articles in the *Times* magazine became more and more quoted as time went on and her weekday column, entitled "Abroad," alternating with that of Arthur Krock, was avidly read. She emerged as one of the world's greatest women journalists and her death in May, 1954, was a great loss to her profession. But the spirit of the woman lives on and her message as the "freedom fighter" is as strong today as when she wrote it.

It was while editing a collection* of Mrs. McCormick's writings on American life, politics and government, that I noticed extraordinary pieces on the Catholic Church—so sharply candid and all the more valuable because of this quality of objectivity. This collection of her writings on the Roman Catholic Church, its papacy, its organization, its consistories, includes her impressions of obscure incidents not usually observed. Many of them are behind-the-scenes reports on how far-reaching is the effort of the Vatican in preserving moral values in every area of society. The writings are for readers of all faiths.

Vatican Journal also contains very nearly all of the spiritual essays Mrs. McCormick wrote to express her concern over the growing power of anti-God forces to crush the rights of human beings. She was greatly concerned about the threat of materialism and its invasion and crippling of the spiritual life of mankind. In days of uncertainty it was refreshing to find her moral convictions stated in terms that could remain unbiased and still retain a strength of challenge to the minds and souls of her readers.

That the world recognized in Mrs. McCormick a truly great journalist is indicated by the quality and number of awards with which she was honored. Among her awards are The New York Evening Post Medal, 1934; Gold Medal of the National Institute of Social Sciences, 1942; the American

* *The World At Home*, Alfred A. Knopf, 1956.

Woman's Association Medal, 1939; Laetare Medal, University of Notre Dame, 1944; Women's National Press Club Achievement Award, 1945; Chi Omega National Achievement Award, 1946; Theodore Roosevelt Distinguished Service Medal, 1950; the William the Silent Award for Journalism, 1952. In 1937 she was awarded the Pulitzer Prize for distinguished foreign correspondence. She held membership in a number of societies, including the National Institute of Arts and Letters. She was a Chevalier of the French Legion of Honor, and a delegate in 1946 and 1948 to the United Nations Educational, Scientific and Cultural Organization conferences. Mrs. McCormick received honorary degrees from many universities and colleges, including Columbia, Dayton, Fordham, New York, and Ohio State universities; Elmira, Lafayette, Manhattan, Middlebury, Mount St. Vincent, Rollins, Smith, Villanova, Wellesley, and Wilson colleges, and the New Jersey College for Women.

I wish to thank those members of the staff of *The New York Times* whose cooperation enabled me to collect Mrs. McCormick's writings. I also wish to express a word of appreciation to Mr. Chester M. Lewis and his staff for their efficient assistance in locating research material; to Elizabeth Ann Flinn for her generous assistance; and a word of tribute to the New York Newspaper Women's Club, New York City, for establishing an annual scholarship in journalism for a graduate girl student, in memory of Anne O'Hare McCormick.

MARION TURNER SHEEHAN

New York City

PART ONE

The Vatican, The Papacy
Church and State

A PAPAL CONSISTORY
AND A POLITICAL DEBUT

July 24, 1921

The fortunate observer of two recent spectacles in Rome was able to see in a single week in June the only two things in a fluid and floundering world that are the same yesterday, today and forever. The two spectacles were the opening of the Italian Parliament and the session of the Papal Consistory, and the two institutions that may be depended upon to survive anything that can happen are human nature and the Catholic Church.

Rome is the divided capital of their opposed and overlapping kingdoms. There is no place where you can see more human nature in a few hours than in a session of the Parliament of Italy, and no place where you are more impressed by the

unchanging tradition of the Catholic Church than at a consistory at the Vatican.

That the two events took place this year in an atmosphere
of what is diplomatically known as accommodation, or *rapprochement* between the two powers which they represent,
only added piquancy to the contrast, and by suggesting that
they may find a practical basis of agreement serves the more
to emphasize their inexorable differences. The eternal inter-
rogation point which the tawny Tiber draws among the famous little hills of Rome has for the past fifty years typified
the attitude of the two empires entrenched upon its opposite
banks. That question is now said to be near an answer. Nobody knows how much reality there is behind the rumors;
but it is evident from newspaper editorials, debates in Parliament and talk in official circles that both sides have felt the
pushing pressure of late events.

The war has demonstrated the hazards and handicaps in
the possession of small and undefended temporal kingdoms,
and has made evident to the Vatican that an Italy more than
ever nationalist will never give up Rome as its capital. It has
also convinced the Quirinal * that whatever governments
come and go, the Papacy remains, and will never, on its part,
give up its claim to absolute independence of any State. But
these positions are not now believed to be irreconcilable, as
once they seemed. Old bitternesses have softened. Anti-clericalism is rather a spent force in Italy, as in France. Everybody
is too busy these days with real perils to be creating bogeys.
Even Mussolini, the Fascist leader, who is emancipated from
all pieties except devotion to Italy, denounces the Free-

---

* Quirinal is the former Papal palace. After confiscation of the Papal states it
was used as a royal palace; it was ceded to Italy by the Papacy in the Latern
Treaty (see footnote, page 60).

masonry which personifies anti-clericalism in Europe as "an enormous screen behind which hide little aims and little men."

He went further in his remarkable first speech in Parliament, in which he advised the Government to follow the lead of the Pope on the question of the mandate in Palestine. "The Latin and imperial tradition of Rome today is represented by Catholicism," he declared. "The only universal idea which exists in Rome is the Vatican. I advance this hypothesis: If the Vatican should definitely renounce its temporal dreams, profane or laic, Italy ought to provide it with all the material assistance possible, because the development of Catholicism in the world is of supreme importance to us."

While not so forthright as Mussolini in avowing their motives, statesmen in all parties profess to recognize at last the reason in the Papal claim that it cannot be at the mercy of continually shifting and unstable parliaments, constrained by their wars and a prey to their transient policies. Watching the growing empire of a Papacy stripped of secular sovereignty, the Quirinal realizes that it is, after all, an empire other than that derived from the possession of Rome and the old States of the Church. Doubtless the Vatican is not blind to this either; the Pope of Rome receives embassies more numerous and more respectful than ever sought the King of Rome.

At any rate, while Benedict XV did not fail to reiterate in the latest consistory the protest of his predecessors against dependence upon the Kingdom of Italy, and while the usurping power must be the first to offer a solution of the problem it has created, this solution is not now held to be incompatible with a purely nominal amount of territory. There is no longer mention of even the ten-mile strip from Rome to the sea, but only of enough ground to house the offices and staff of the

Holy See—the Vatican and Lateran palaces and the Papal villa at Castelgandolfo, sites even now extraterritorial under the Law of Guarantees* and comprising hardly more than a gentleman's estate.

But however the two courts may come together, they must always remain worlds apart. I watched the two events which brought them into the same focus with a sense that the circumstances that are forcing them to a working adjustment have also widened the gulf that forever divides them. The Italian Parliament represents what the war has done to modern States. The overdeveloped human nature of the Italian people makes it a somewhat exaggerated example, but all national congresses at the present moment are more or less clamorous with the same conflicts of opinion, the same confusions, bewilderments and angry impotence. The consistory, on the other hand, seemed to testify that the war has done nothing at all to the ancient Church. The nervous agitations and uncertainties of Montecitorio are felt in every seat of Government in the world except the Vatican. That maintains its steady and unflustered tranquillity, its uninterrupted rule and procedure, a ritual never out of fashion, like the dress of its religious orders, because never in fashion. I suppose there never was a time when the sight of undisputed authority was more startling.

The opening of the twenty-sixth Parliament of Italy was a historic occasion, the first in which was represented all—or nearly all—of her rightful kingdom. Only fifty years ago an aggregation of warring States, she is at last, though reduced from her ancient power as the greatest of empires, occupying the frontiers carved by nature, by tradition, and by Napoleon. There was great demand for seats in the galleries, and my

* Law of Guarantees, refer to Page 29.

first impression, as I squeezed into my corner in a crowded tribune and looked about at the spectators and the gathering Senators and Deputies, was that Italians look more like a nation than almost any other people. In the mass they are not only a good-looking but a homegeneous race, enough alike to lend the same kind of harmony to their assemblies that a city like Paris achieves by specializing on different varieties of the same style of architecture. The members of Parliament appeared no better or no worse, no more or less distinguished, than the same body in England, in France, or in the United States. But they did look Italian, and thus, in spite of all their divergences, more racially unified than similar assemblies elsewhere.

No one can accuse the Italian Court of being a demonstrative monarchy. It is the quietest and most unostentatious thing in the country. Nobody in Italy makes less trouble than the King, who shuns publicity, avoids any appearance of interfering with the Government, and parades his royalty only when he is dragged out of seclusion by necessity. The opening of Parliament is one of the rare occasions when he appears in Rome. He comes to the Chamber in a good deal of traditional state, in a crystal chariot drawn by white horses with jeweled harnesses, heralded by bugles and gorgeous outriders and all the other glittering circus trappings which monarchies really pay a king to furnish.

But having delivered the show to the people in the streets, Victor Emmanuel came into the Chamber quietly, in the gray uniform of a colonel, the grand dukes and officers with him in similar garb. A delightful old General standing next to me in the tribune was much more glorious. At the same moment the Queen,* her daughters and the hereditary prince

* The Princess Elena of Montenegro.

took their places in the gallery above, very simply attired also, but as personally decorative a royal group as any monarchy can furnish. The King, never a commanding figure, and impatient of the strut and pose by which many little men try to assume greatness, was dwarfed by the size of the throne, and when he kicked away the red velvet footstool provided for him he looked not unlike an unhappy small boy dangling his legs in a chair too big for him.

The opening of Parliament in England, where the King has no more power than in Italy, is much more of a royal pageant, colorful, feudal, heavily embroidered by tradition. The English like to be called "my subjects." I have heard many of them proclaim themselves "British subjects" with a good deal of pride. The more democratic Italians do not like the title at all. The King never once referred to "subjects" in his discourse. He referred to the people as citizens, which is the only designation I have ever heard an Italian use when he spoke of himself in relation to the monarchy.

The speech itself was dignified in its simplicity, in its well-turned phrases, in its compact brevity. Probably prepared by the Prime Minister, it was an admirable document, with just enough emphasis on the return of the lost provinces and just enough grave insistence on the problems that face united and reunited Italy. For the student of contrasts, it was not uninteresting to observe that the most vociferous cheers for the King came from the benches of the Popular Party, which no doubt saw in his demand for educational reform and legislation for the small proprietors the Government's adoption of the principal planks in the Popular platform.

But more interesting than the speech or the King was the sudden emergence of the new party of the Extreme Right in the calling of the roll. The Republican Fascisti and most of the Socialists absented themselves from the opening session. They object to answering the roll call with *Giuro!*—"I swear"—on an occasion which makes the parliamentary oath like a vow of allegiance to royalty. But the small group of Fascisti who were present could not allow their entry into the Chamber to pass unnoticed. They made a perfectly legitimate demonstration against the name of Misiano, the communist deserter from the army, who was able to keep his place through the last session of Parliament. They loudly disapproved of several other Deputies. "Down with Austria!" they thundered when the Premier came to the names of any of the nine Slav or German members returned from a section of the Redenta.* And when the brief session was over and the King and his aids rose to go amid the "vivas" of the assemblage, they started the Fascist hymn, *Giovanezza,* or "Youth," and would not be stopped by their embarrassed and conventional elders. They were not to be awed or subdued by royalty or old decorums, or any of the musty traditions that smother initiative and self-expression.

They kept on demonstrating their own insurgence in particular, and the present insurgence of human nature in general, during all those early sessions of the Legislature which are devoted to the responses of the various parties to the address from the throne. I was lucky enough to be in the Chamber during the tumultuous meeting of June 21, when there were four first speeches of a character to lash into frenzy the inheritors of the political passions in the land. As a show, the occasion was priceless. I have never seen quite so much energy and anger unleashed in a single place. There were moments when the high room actually shook with sound, as in a thunderstorm, when everybody in it howled at once,

* A section of northern Italy formerly held by the Austro-Hungarian Empire.

stamped and frothed and beat the air with upraised fists, rushed back and forth in an indescribable confusion of deafening racket and crazy motion. The tinkle of the silly little bell which takes the place of the speaker's gavel in the Italian Chamber was as completely lost in the clamor as was the voice of the President, de Nicola. No moderator could still that tempest.

Benito Mussolini, founder and leader of the Fascisti, was among the parliamentary débutants; and in one of the best political speeches I have ever heard, a little swaggering but caustic, powerful and telling, he called upon the Socialists to disarm their spirits. Turati, the Socialist leader, in an even more impressive appeal the next day, called upon both extremes of the Chamber for a spiritual truce in the interests of the country. But there was no sign or promise of any kind of disarmament in the scene I witnessed.

To an American who had listened to the debate in the United States Senate on the League of Nations and the Treaty of Versailles, the first speech of Buratono, leader of the extremists in the Socialist Party, did not seem very intemperate. But from his first words, when he demanded that the Government should demonstrate that the new Chamber was any different from the old, and the Fascisti shouted, "But yes! But yes! We are here!" he talked against a tumult. And when he affirmed that his party had never blasphemed the country, but only did not make a speculation of patriotism, the floods burst in earnest. No one was seriously hurt in the mêlée that followed, but for a time the middle of the Chamber was the arena of several hand-to-hand encounters between the uncontrollable spirits of the Extreme Right and the Extreme Left. The Socialist member of the Cabinet tried to interfere and left the Chamber in a huff at the rebuke of Giolitti. President de Nicola retired from his futile bell-ringing and suspended the session in an indignation that made no impression on indignations so much more furious than his.

The atmosphere was not much calmer when the sitting was resumed. The speeches of the German Deputy, Walter, and the Slav Deputy, Wilfan, suave but insolent protests against annexation to Italy, which roused even the crouching Giolitti to a sharp lunge of anger, were not calculated to pour oil on the troubled waters. During the latter speech, I feared the young Fascist Deputy from Trieste, Signor Giunta, would have a stroke of apoplexy. I admire the Fascisti. Their illimitable energy is the miracle of a weary world. It is easy to sympathize with their patriotic exasperation. Just now they are engaged in a literal and successful fight against high prices, which gives them a new claim upon the gratitude of a cowed and helpless public.

But it must be admitted that some of them, that day in Parliament, acted like nothing so much as spoiled children in a howling temper. If they keep up their raging pace, they will either die of physical exhaustion themselves or exhaust and kill the Parliament. Not even an Italian Legislature can function in that hullabaloo. A fat Italian, who must have been in New York as long as six months, leaned over to shout to me in the midst of the storm: "These are crazy people. We don't do things like this in America, do we?"

The young man at my left bristled, "All Parliaments are the same, aren't they?" he asked, defensively. "Look at England."

"Well, nearly, but not quite," I had to answer. "They all talk as wildly, but only the Italians seem to listen so furiously."

To turn from a humanity as untamed and turbulent as this

to the solemn restraints and ancient disciplines represented
by the consistory is a little like stepping from one world into
another. Perhaps it is. I tried to formulate the difference between them as the contrast between the perpetual transitions
of the democratic and the perpetual stability of the aristo-
cratic system. But I could not make all the facts fit into that
easy formula. As a spectacle, the consistory naturally had the
best of it. The Sala Regia* at the Vatican is not large, but it
is of a rather overpowering magnificence. A great tapestry,
perhaps from the design of Raphael, hung behind the Papal
throne at one end. Other priceless stuffs of the High Renaissance covered the three tribunes, one for the diplomats, another for the nobles of the Papal court, and a third for the
relatives and guests of the prelates who received the Red Hat.
The rest of us who had managed to get in stood around the
walls, behind a line of decorative but not very military guards.
Every one was in the picture, a crowded and animated medieval canvas in which one felt strangely and beautifully at
home. The women were black-gowned and black-veiled, but
the men, in the eye-filling costumes of all the Papal orders,
from the elegant gallants in black velvet capes and white
starched ruffs to the fascinating swashbucklers in slashed scarlet, stirred vain regrets for the days of the unextinguished
male.

The purple and crimson trains of high prelates swished by.
The diplomats in their tribune were heavy with gold lace
and loaded with orders. M. Jonnart, the first envoy of France
to the Papal court since the separation of Church and State,
made his first official appearance. He looks like the best type
of French bourgeois, florid, stocky, steady and competent, his
knees a little rusty as he bent them to the Pope. At the en-

* The Sala Regia is known as the Hall of Royalty in the Vatican Palace.

trance of the English Ambassador, Count de Salis, someone behind me wondered how he had enjoyed the criticism of English rule in Palestine in the address of His Holiness at the secret consistory, a bit of plain speaking more relished by the Fascisti than by the English Catholics in Rome.

The Cardinals swept past, each new prince of the Church between two old ones. They were attended by gorgeous hat-bearers and preceded by giants in the rainbow uniforms of the Swiss Guard. The whole effect was more opulent and aristo-cratic than anything I have ever seen. But the new princes themselves had no air of lordliness. They were all rather old men, and they looked what most of them were, no doubt— churchmen who had come up through the ranks from humble beginnings and to whom these late honors were not very im-portant. And for all the high panoply of the setting, the gathering of spectators in the Sala Regia was much more mixed and democratic than that which had watched the open-ing of Parliament from the more exclusive tribunes of Monte-citorio. Peasants, students, young priests, travelers from the ends of the earth, crowded against Italian princes and Papal counts. The guard that very slackly held the line was informal and friendly, leaving convenient gaps for the visitor to see through, obligingly unaware of the short of stature who ven-tured in front of them, and behaving generally with a human irregularity unthinkable in the statue-like cuirassiers of the King. The ceremony was a curious mixture of pomp and simplicity, of discipline and laissez-faire. It did not sustain any theory of established aristocracy and iron law. The mold was evidently old and easy enough not to chafe.

The sound of silver trumpets in the distance heralded the approach of the Pope. The sound is rather unearthly, high and piercingly sweet, and its effect was to lay a silence so loud that it shouted upon the whispering throng in the Sala Regia and the crowded corridor outside.

Benedict XV is no more impressive to look at than Victor Emmanuel. In his insignificant figure and rather expressionless face there is no majesty, spiritual or secular. But as he was borne into the consistory chamber in his uplifted golden chair, those ineffable waving fans of white peacock feathers somehow hedged him in and brushed him aside, so that the man inside the Pope did not matter at all. He was lost in something impersonal, perpetual, obliterating. It was the Papacy one saw moving in the hush, swallowing up good Popes, bad Popes and indifferent Popes, and surviving them all. I saw the colors of the French Republic, stretched across the stiff shirt front of its representative, go down before it. Holland bowed, and Albania, and the stiffly gilded court uniform of the British Empire. An Italian Senator, who very evidently meant to stand with a respectful inclination, was forced to his knees. There is something subjugating in the only unbroken tradition left in the world.

The ceremony itself was not long. The Pontiff placed upon the head of each new prince of the Church in turn the same red hat, an enormous crimson plaque, that has made centuries of cardinals. He read a brief address, naming a number of new bishops, in a thin and nervous voice. He was borne out again in the same state and stillness in which he entered. The cardinals proceeded to the adjoining chapel, the Sistine, and prostrated themselves before the altar, under the titanic masterpiece of Michelangelo. It was easy to imagine one's self in the sixteenth century or in the twenty-sixth, but difficult to realize the twentieth. The clamor of parliaments seemed a long way off, and all the convulsions, revulsions and conflicts of the world. To see something perfectly calm and static

when everything whirls, to feel an authority absolutely assured when no supremacy is safe, was a quite incredible experience.

It is not as if the Vatican can be oblivious to the tumults
of the time or has no part in them. I caught sight of an Arab
and a New Zealander in the Sistine, and recognized among
the assisting prelates a Spaniard, a German, an Oriental, a
Canadian and a South American. One has to come to Rome
to realize that the Vatican goes everywhere and knows everything. It has a purely business and administrative organization that functions so quietly that no one quite appreciates
the extent of it. There are over 300,000,000 * Catholics in the
world and about 1,500 organized states, or dioceses, working
missions in every wilderness and desert island, a vast educational, philanthropic and diplomatic system, all more or less
directed from some office in Rome. The Vatican has been
dealing for ages with racial problems like those that swamped
the Paris Peace Conference. Its international business makes
that of the Secretariat of the League of Nations seem parochial. And the monstrous thing is run without fuss. That is
what distinguishes it most from the fuming and distracted
administrations of the times.

In the Italian Chamber of Deputies the Roman Question†
looms big and appears as controversial and important as it
doubtless is. From the consistory, it looks like a dispute over
sixpence by the owner of the moon.

* It is now estimated that there are approximately 484,000,000 Catholics in the
world and about 2,000 organized dioceses.
† Matters of issue between the Holy See and the civil government consequent
upon the seizure of Rome by the Piedmontese in 1870. The main difficulty
concerned the position of the Popes who, as independent sovereign persons
forcibly deprived of their territory, confined themselves within the Vatican.
The Roman Question was settled by the Lateran Treaty (see footnote, page 60).

2

BENEDICT XV
AND PAPAL PRESTIGE

February 12, 1922

Benedict XV, the fourth Pope since the Kingdom of Italy took possession of Rome, was the first for whose death the Italian Government lowered its flags to half-mast in token of mourning.

That gesture of Italy is significant. It draws attention to qualities in the dead Pontiff that were not generally recognized during his life. Benedict was little known and little considered until he died. Now a curiously clouded personality and a singularly overshadowed career suddenly emerge into the light of appraisal and take on new dimensions. His separately small and quiet achievements all at once add up to such a sum of accomplishment that one begins to wonder if in the insignificant figure of the late Pope the world may not have lost a great man.

We are accustomed to the sight of Popes moving across the stage of history. They are the only leading characters always in the picture. Like the ancient Chair of the Fisherman hidden under Bernini's tortured bronze in the overpowering tribune of St. Peter's, they are among the few historic legends that survive as facts. It is inevitable that the occupant of that Chair should often be lost in it. Only a very great Pope can escape extinction in an office constrained to majesty by its power in the past and its unabated claim in the present to spiritual sovereignty.

Benedict XV seemed one of the negative Popes, dwarfed by his position and overpowered by the events of his time. One saw him at public functions in the Vatican, drooping under his tiara, dwindling within his embroidered state, plainly bored and burdened by his augustness. He appeared to the casual eye as one merely carrying on the Papal tradition dutifully, resignedly, even competently, but certainly not animating or decorating it. He made no appeal to the imagination—a little man, awkward, tired, sallow, one shoulder slightly higher than the other, with no eloquence, no radiance, no personal charm. His reign saw the world torn by war and unplacated by peace. During the conflict he pleased no one, and all his efforts to end it resulted in failure. He was as one talking against tempests, a futile preacher of dead and powerless platitudes. He managed to achieve neither the picturesqueness of the pastoral simplicity of Pius X nor the impressiveness of the brilliant old age of Leo XIII.

Yet now that he is dead he begins to grow larger and more definite. His accomplishment looks greater than that of either of his predecessors. After his seven years of apparent impotence he is suddenly discovered to have left the Papacy with more prestige than it has enjoyed for a hundred years. While war raged he succeeded in reconciling the old political enemies of the Holy See and in drawing envoys from most of the Courts of the earth to seek his counsel. The Italy that in the secret pact * of London excluded him from the Peace Conference came home from Paris chastened and disillusioned to seek the friendship of the Vatican. "It is a pity we could not have sent the Pope to Paris," said one embittered Italian statesman. "He is turning out to be the only diplomat we have."

"Italy needs the Church more than the Church needs Italy," remarked the late Pope himself more than a year ago in an interview with two Americans who ventured to bring up the subject of the rumored *rapprochement* between the Italian Government and the Holy See.

They were told afterward that they had trodden on forbidden ground, and that only an American and an outsider would have had the temerity to broach a topic so delicate in the presence of the Pope. It was well known that there had been conversations between Cardinal Gasparri and Premiers Nitti and Giolitti, and that various understandings had been reached in regard to Government restrictions that had hampered the Vatican in the transaction of ecclesiastical business. Benedict, on his side, had lifted the ban against the visits of Catholic Sovereigns to the Quirinal, and had probably staved off national disaster in Italy by permitting Catholics to take part in the general elections. It was evident that unofficial relations between the Vatican and the Quirinal were better

* Orlando, Premier of Italy; Clemenceau, Premier of France; and Lloyd George, British Prime Minister, agreed to exclude Vatican representation at the Versailles Peace Conference.

than they had ever been before. But officially there was no *rapprochement* at all, and it is a *faux pas* to mention anything but the obvious to the rulers of even spiritual States.

His Holiness treated the lapse gently, however. He did not give the impression of being a man of humor, but his keen eyes twinkled, and if he did not commit himself beyond a carefully phrased suggestion that it was the province of the usurper to find a solution of the Roman Question that would be acceptable to the usurped, he did encourage the expression of an American opinion on a very controversial subject.

In fact, Benedict encouraged his visitors to the expression of views on all subjects, controversial or otherwise. And it is proof of his simplicity—or yours!—that you found yourself telling him quite freely what you thought. No Pope, of course, ever receives correspondents as such or gives interviews to the newspapers. But it was no use trying to interview the late Pontiff in one's most private capacity. He always interviewed his interviewers. He darted from point to point, probing the mind of his visitor. When he first assumed office he instructed his Secretary that he did not wish to read clippings, as had been the custom of his predecessors; he wished to read newspapers. The same desire to savor for himself all sorts of divergent and uncensored views and all varieties of information was typical of his conversation.

As I look back upon that audience and recall the number of unrelated subjects he was able to touch upon in less than half an hour, how frankly he talked and questioned, how open and fluid was his mind and how eager his intellectual curiosity, I regain the impression so strong at the time—that Benedict was astonishingly unknown to the outside world. No one who saw him only in public got any idea of his vivacity, his roving intelligence, his vivid penetration. To observe him at large audiences or at public functions after having engaged him in private conversation was like looking at a lamp quenched or a window heavily shuttered. The impassivity he assumed on such occasions, like the lack of expression in all his photographs, belied alike the vigor of his short frame and the robustness of his personality.

I remember his quick, staccato stride as he crossed his library to meet us on the morning of our reception; the swift glance with which he greeted and took us in; his curt gesture to the attendant to close the door and leave us alone. I do not remember the room at all. In the presence of Benedict XV the eye and the mind had no chance to wander. He had the man of the world's ease with strangers that puts them at their ease, and at once drew us into two armchairs facing his with a manner that suggested the friendly host and not at all the Sovereign Pontiff.

I imagine that no recent Pope took his office more seriously or himself more simply than Benedict XV. When I saw Pius X he seemed oppressed by his pontificate, overcome by mighty powers and mighty responsibilities. Benedict XV was less conscious of himself as Pope in his unofficial moments. Pius was paternal, touching, himself moved by great spiritual passions and pities. Benedict had none of the pontifical manner. He was natural, responsive, of a business-like directness. His steady seriousness was unlightened by any of the famous wit of Leo XIII or the soft laughter of so many old Bishops. He had none of the marks of mellowing age. He looked hardy, young, vigilant.

The Pope went on to question us about America. He was curious as to the real causes of what seemed to him the reversal of public sentiment in regard to the League of Nations, which, perhaps because he felt himself to be not without a part in its formulation, he called "a great conception." I was told by a Vatican official that no one in Europe had more faith in President Wilson than the Pope, or more deeply regretted his defeat by the Senate. He expressed concern over Mr. Wilson's health, and knew the names and the politics of the candidates in the electoral campaign then in progress. Altogether, in spite of his ignorance of English, he showed a knowledge of American politics very unusual in a foreigner, and exceeding that of any one I met in Italy except ex-Premier Orlando. He said that he was struck by the diminishing political strength of socialism in the United States at a time when it was almost overpowering the Governments of Europe. He prophesied that the force of circumstances would prevent America from escaping her destiny.

He wanted to hear our impression of the observance of the fiftieth anniversary of the union of Italy, which we had witnessed a short time before, and when we replied with truth that it seemed a very perfunctory and unpopular festival, the Pope expressed more anxiety than gratification. He had no reason to regret a celebration that had been frowned upon by the King and ignored by most of the people for fear of offending the Pope. But he recognized, as he said, that it was not a happy time in Italy for festivals.

He mentioned the occupation of the factories by the workers of Milan and the continual procession of strikes and street fights that made travel in Italy at that time something of an adventure.

"But Italy is not and never will be Bolshevist," he declared with energy. "What you see is a flame that will go out. There is no intellectual foundation for Bolshevism here. The people are deeply conservative."

The Pope based his conviction on considerable knowledge of the Italian industrial classes. Bologna has been for years a storm center of anarchy, the scene of more organized revolt than any place in Italy. As Archbishop of that turbulent see, Benedict XV devoted most of his time and attention to the welfare of the workers. He knew the Italian workingman, his real grievances against an almost feudal society, his dangerous impulsiveness and the saving common sense of his second thoughts. He was a native of the industrial north, a member of an old and noble family, it is true, but saved by his episcopal experience and his searching intelligence from taking the upper or outer view of the social problems of his time.

It was evident from his interest that these problems were what chiefly attracted and engrossed him. The late Pope was undoubtedly possessed by the belief that the thing he was ordained to do in a world of war was to make peace. He had carefully refrained during the war from any action that might weaken his claim to be the arbitrator of conflicts. He passed no judgments on the belligerents except those protests against incontrovertible outrages like the sinking of the *Lusitania,* the bombing of churches, the slaughter of non-combatants. But he realized that the consequences of the war were more devastating than the war itself, and that a military peace was a kind of cosmic sarcasm so long as there was neither economic nor social peace.

In the course of the talk, when he was referring to the activities of American welfare agencies, he jumped up from his chair to fetch from the other side of the room some photographs of himself taken with a group of members of the Knights of Columbus, who had made a pilgrimage to Rome during the preceding Summer. "That's an unusual picture of a Pope, isn't it?" he asked with a smile. "I think it is the first time the Holy Father has ever been photographed with a company of laymen—and, of course, they were Americans!"

The Pope introduced many other topics in the course of the audience, but since it is impossible to report him literally I can only present a few odd scraps from the lively patch-work of his talk, with the hope of conveying at least a sugges-tion of how different he was from what he appeared or was supposed to be. It is presumptuous with such slight materials to attempt to revise a general impression, but there are so few "close-up" views of Benedict XV, he was so obscured behind clouds of war on the one hand and clouds of incense on the other, that any passing glimpse behind the screen has a cer-tain power of illumination. As his death discloses that a Pontiff who in a great time seemed to be doing little in reality accomplished much, so anyone who met him face to face felt the dynamic force and purpose burning under his im-mobile public manner.

Benedict was less understood but better liked than Pius X in a Roman society, both ecclesiastical and secular, that loves a diplomat better than anything on earth, and an aris-tocrat next to a diplomat. The combination of the two is irresistible! Yet Rome, outside of the officials of his household, knew no more of the Pope than New York knew of him. He was more retiring than Popes must be by the restrictions of circumstance, but he went about his business—his business of knowing this rent and ragged world, of patching it up and drawing the seams together by small stitches wherever he could, of strengthening always the power of that spiritual kingdom which he ruled—with a still and imperturbable con-centration.

Benedict may or may not have been a great Pope. He had

two qualities in a great degree—prudence and patience. These are not the qualities of genius; but in times like these they are perhaps more mollifying to the world's angers—and to the wrath of God which Pontiffs as profoundly faithful as he was must first fear—than more brilliant and subjugating gifts.

Before another election, if the new Pope is as skillful as the last, the Roman Question, which at present seems to bar non-Italians from the supreme office in the Catholic Church, may be as dead as the Austrian veto. Meantime Cardinal Maffi, known as "the Liberal," the great social reformer, whose influence has already outgrown the moribund old town of Pisa, is the outstanding churchman in Italy. The singular thing is that in any event the statesmanship of the Pope of Rome seems to matter more to the world than to the Church. The Papacy is apparently impregnable, time-proof and Pope-proof. But the world gropes for wisdom in some high place.

3

THE AGE-OLD ISSUE
STIRS ROME

October 10, 1926

Rome remains a disputed capital. It is a small town, as cities go. The Seven Hills are little hills. From any one of them, in the smokeless air, you can see it all—terraces of faded tile roofs, blond domes, innumerable housetop gardens; Titus and Victor Emmanuel on this side, Peter on the other; all colossal, all crowded together, and all claiming possession of a capital too small to be divided and yet forever destined to division.

It is the problem and, as far as one can gather, even the pride of Rome that it is the inevitable center of two kingdoms, one new and one old, one national and one international, and that both, the dispossessor and the dispossessed, rule and must somehow continue to rule side by side. I think it enjoys the dilemma. With far more relish than heat it puts the poser known as the Roman Question: Where but in Rome can Italy have its capital; where but on the tomb of the first Pope can the Papacy have its throne? And how can these two Roman sovereignties be maintained and satisfied?

The conflict waged for three-quarters of a century between Italy and the Holy See for the possession of the Eternal City —on the one hand the natural capital of the kingdom and on the other belonging to the Popes since the time of Charlemagne, if not from the time of Constantine—gains a new liveliness from the intrusion of Fascism upon the scene and from the determination of Mussolini to solve the knottiest of all the problems inherited from the old Government.

It does not matter that one power in Rome represents the Kingdom of Heaven; the Kingdom of Heaven on earth requires offices bigger, more concentrated and more independent than does the small and strictly localized Kingdom of Italy. Rome is still substanially a pontifical city, as any traveler can see who moves among palaces, churches, bridges, fountains, aqueducts, gardens, erected and embellished by an endless dynasty of Popes. It does not matter that no Italian, least of all the exalted Italian of the present moment, would ever consent that the capital of Italy should be anything less than the center of Christendom. The paradox of the passion of Romanity revived by the *fasces,* the Roman salute, the constant evocation of "Roma Augusta," is that it extends also to the Pontifex Maximus,* who kept Rome a capital from Caesar to Victor Emmanuel and who must remain in Rome if only to add to the prestige of the Italian capital. The

---

* Supreme Pontiff, a title which dates from the time of the priesthood of ancient Rome and which later became inseparable from the office of Emperor.

Fascists are willing to divide Rome, if necessary, to keep its glory whole!

I shall never forget the gasp that reduced to silence the most unmanageable and tumultuous parliamentary session I ever attended when a voice heard for the first time in the Italian National Assembly made the following declaration:

"There is one problem that rises above all these contingent problems. It is the historic problem of the relations between Italy and the Vatican.

"I affirm that the Latin and imperial tradition of Rome is today represented by Catholicism.

"If, as Mommsen said twenty-five or thirty years ago, one cannot remain in Rome without a universal idea, I believe and declare that the only universal idea that exists in Rome today is that which radiates from the Vatican."

Until June, 1921, when this declaration was made, no one had dared for fifty years to open in the Italian Chamber the question that since the occupation of Rome in 1870 had divided and paralyzed the country. The speaker was Benito Mussolini, and the occasion was the first speech made by the first Fascist in the same Parliament that less than a year and a half later, in November, 1922, he was to enter as head of the Government. On that later occasion he made another precedent. "May God help me," he concluded that scourging of the Chamber that heralded a precedent-smashing régime—"may God help me to carry to a victorious end my arduous task."

That was the first time that a Prime Minister had ever invoked in modern Italy the name of God. A people as used to public piety as ourselves, accustomed to Congresses, political conventions and even bigger and better business rallies opened and closed with respectful admonitions to Providence,

can never understand the thoroughgoing abolition of the
Deity decreed by Latin Governments when they begin to
"secularize." The sensation caused when Mussolini introduced the Vatican and the Almighty to a shocked Parliament
shows the gulf that had to be bridged before the issue between the Kingdom and the Papacy could even be discussed.
The gulf was only artificial—political stage scenery—as is
evident from the amiable conversations on the subject now
taking place. During the past few weeks I have interviewed
high and authoritative representatives of both the Church
and the Government, and have heard Roman Cardinals echoing the doubts and perplexities of Cabinet Ministers. There
is on the right bank of the Tiber, among rulers of the
Church, a recognition of the difficulties of the Government
which would amaze faraway Catholics who think there is
nothing more to the solution of the Roman Question than
the restoration to the Popes of as much of their stolen
territory as is necessary to render them independent of the
secular power. And there is on the left bank, among spokesmen for the State, an understanding of the grounds of the
Papal claim for temporal power which would equally surprise
those who cannot see any connection between spiritual authority and territorial independence.

There is especially in the Palazzo Chigi a keen desire
to remove the rankling irritation of the passive resistance to
Italy represented by the "imprisonment" of the Pope. It is
Mussolini's dearest ambition to be the statesman already
given preeminence by the strongest of his predecessors, old
Francesco Crispi, when he said: "The greatest Italian statesman will be the one who will solve the Roman Question."

Will he solve it? He has missed no opportunity to create
an atmosphere favorable to solution. From his first speech in

Parliament to the present moment the ex-Socialist has labored with the fervor of an evangelist to restore religion to his country.

A new tone in respect to the Church marks the Italian press. Catholic Italy used to be like a man whose wife and mother refused to speak to each other. Now that unnatural strain is over. For the first time since the Papal reign, Cardinals walk about the Roman streets and enjoy with other Romans the incomparable sunsets from the Pincio.

It is not many years since an Italian statesman would have considered it suicidal to propose giving a slice of Rome to the Pope, or since it was almost heresy for a Catholic to suggest that the Pope could accept such a slice in lieu of his former sovereignty. Now a Government commission is at work revising the "Law of Guarantees," passed in 1871 to regularize the occupation of Papal territory by the grandfather of the present King, and to protect the person and rights of the Pope in that "enjoyment" of the Vatican allowed him by the Kingdom of Italy.

Every Pontiff since, from Pius IX to Pius XI, has refused to recognize this law, to benefit by its compensations or to renounce any of the rights which it abrogates. On the ground that since Italy is the usurper, from Italy must come the formula of redress and restitution, the Pope even now declines to be officially represented in the present revision.

It is often asked abroad why a régime so favorable to the Church should be the object of frequent attacks in the Vatican organ, the *Osservatore Romano*. Why is this journal so immune from the general censorship that it has grown from a little regarded ecclesiastical organ to one of the most important and widely read papers in Italy and the one most widely quoted in the foreign press?

The *Osservatore* prints nothing not approved by the Papal Secretary of State—and prints the only protests against the abuses and restrictions of Fascism. The explanation, on one side, is that the Vatican must demonstrate its independence of any Italian Goverment, friendly or unfriendly; and on the other, that the Government acknowledges the international status of the Holy See and will not endanger the possible settlement of the Roman Question by any limitation of its present liberty.

Such assertion and such forbearance, singular in Fascist Italy, illustrate better than anything else the excellence of present relations between Church and State. Does the rapid progress toward reconciliation mean that reconciliation is at hand? I ventured to put this question to Cardinal Gasparri and to Mussolini, the two protagonists in the present round of the old contest. Both answers were identically non-committal. "I hope so!" said the Duce, so vigorously that it sounded like a promise. "I hope so!" echoed the Cardinal.

Another Cardinal, a papal diplomat of wide experience, pointed out obstacles in the way of settlement that would never occur to the simple lay mind, but expressed the opinion that the time was opportune and that every effort should be made to meet the difficulties now, while Italy was governed by a man with the will and power to act. "Such an opportunity may not occur again," he said.

Still another prince of the Church, when told that a Government representative had complained that the Vatican could not decide what terms it could accept, declared that such a statement was nonsense. "The question can be settled," said this Cardinal, whose views are significant because he is supposed to be charged with exploring the possibilities of solution on behalf of the Church. "It could be settled to-morrow. The Government knows exactly what would satisfy the Vatican."

Signor Federzoni, the able, moderate and universally trusted Minister of the Interior was questioned because he is credited with being as keen as his chief to clear the title to the ownership of Rome. The members of the Mussolini Cabinet are always overworked and overtired, and Federzoni was as fagged and driven as all the others. It was pure good nature that made him explain so patiently the gravity and delicacy of the issues involved in the Roman Question. It is simple only from a distance; the nearer it is approached the more complicated it appears. "It is not the kind of difficulty that can be settled in a day, or a year," he said. "Time, after all, is the best negotiator."

Indeed, the impression gained from a canvass of competent opinion on both sides of the Tiber is that in spite of the good will and optimism of statesmen and ecclesiastics and constant rumors that the Pope is about to leave the Vatican— to go to Assisi, for instance, during the Franciscan Year—the problem is not yet anywhere near solution. This conclusion is not shared by most observers, who predict an early settle-ment on the ground that when the spirit of reconciliation exists the reconciling formula must soon be found. They forget that this is no ordinary opposition, to be conquered by ordinary compromises. It involves the invisible; deals with rights so sacrosanct to their custodians that they are afraid to modify them.

These rights have been declared "imprescriptible" as late as the present year by a Pope whose benevolence toward the intentions of the present Government does not prevent him from reaffirming as rigidly as any of his predecessors that "the divine origin and nature of our power as well as the sacred right of the community of the faithful scattered throughout the world require that the sacred power should be independent of all human authority and should not be subject to human laws, even though these laws claim to protect the liberty of the Roman Pontiff by assistance or guarantees."

It is true that "temporal power" is no longer thought of except as a sign of independence. If new Italy recognizes that as the capital of Christendom prestige, pilgrims and profit accrue to Rome, the Popes have also learned that their spiritual sovereignty has not suffered and that their moral power has increased since they ceased to be the secular rulers of an insignificant kingdom. They wish now only to be neither subject nor guest of any nation; to have extraterritorial space only to house the Vatican offices and diplomats accredited to the Holy See. The outlet to the sea is not emphasized. Airplanes have altered even ecclesiastical ideas of freedom of communication.

These demands public opinion in Italy, so far as it is audible, seems now disposed to grant.

But the real crux of the problem, now as in the past, is the matter of guarantees. What is to give to any solution of the Roman Question a sanction more stable than that which the Popes have already repudiated?

No nation willingly consents to the control of other nations within her territory. Perhaps the League of Nations offers a way out of this difficulty. It has been suggested that when an agreement between Italy and the Holy See is finally reached formal registration in Geneva will give it international sanction, or that Italy might simply notify the powers that an arrangement with the Vatican had been concluded.

I say "finally reached," because no such epilogue is imminent. The impatience of the Fascist Government and the impetuosity of Mussolini are vain before an institution that believes in eternity—and acts on that belief. All Popes are cautious, and Pius XI, who has also the temperament of a scholar, is the most cautious of Popes. Even in the timeless atmosphere of Papal Rome, where nothing hurries, he is noted for his habit of studying questions from all angles and coming very slowly to decisions.

The present Pontiff is more vigorous, more alert and more assured than he seemed after his election four years ago; but one who talks with him today comes away with the impression that other things preoccupy him far more than does the Roman Question. He can afford to wait; he might even prefer to pass the problem on to his successor. The Vatican attitude is that a settlement must be so final and definitive that the *status quo* is better than a solution that does not provide for all future possibilities.

It must be added that there is a great body of opinion, within the Church and outside, that considers no solution the best solution. It argues that the claims of the Popes and the Kings of Italy are irreconcilable, and that as Papal sovereignty in the so-called "Apostolic City" cannot be real or absolute except in name it is better to continue a protest that preserves at least the moral independence of the Papacy and saves both Church and State from any suspicion of being influenced the one by the other.

Exponents of this view contend that so long as there is any claim to temporal power, or the question remains open, it is necessary for the Pope to be an Italian, while at the same time he cannot be, as he never has been, Italian in the national sense. With a settlement, the same necessity no longer exists; and they ask whether it would be a benefit to introduce national rivalry for the honor of the Papacy into conclaves now free of that consideration.

The two present powers in divided Rome have not much in common; but neither admits anything to be impossible— the one because it is so old and the other because it is so young.

The Roman Question is soluble and will finally be solved. It is not safe to gamble against the speed or resourcefulness of Mussolini. But if, as the wisest Romans say, time is set- tling the question, and only time can bring the settlement to a conclusion, the chances of the Popes to see it settled are rather better than are the chances of the Fascists.

4

ANCIENT ROTA IS UNMOVED
BY ATTACKS

January 2, 1927

Old and accustomed to controversy is the Holy Roman Rota.
Once the High Court of Christendom celebrated as the
"Asylum of Justice" and the "Roman Areopagus" by the
exuberant chroniclers of the Renaissance, it now functions
quietly in a little old palace overshadowed by the Quirinal,
forgotten by the world until the dissension caused by one of
its decisions pushes it again into secular prominence. Like
ecclesiastical Rome itself, which governs a world empire in
easy contrast with its straining Fascist neighbor, the Rota is
characteristically undisturbed by arguments either attacking
or defending its competence and its judgment.

The inquirer who questions Roman prelates and doctors of
canon law hears expressions of regret that the Marlborough-

Vanderbilt case, for instance, was ever brought before the Rota, which as a court of appeal, it is explained, is obligated to pronounce judgment when judgment is demanded by regular legal process. He hears expressions of polite surprise that those who do not recognize the authority of the Catholic Church should be agitated by decisions that bind only Catholics and state only the Catholic point of view. But what really whets the interest of ecclesiastical Rome is not outside opinion, or the position of the persons involved, but the unusual points of canon law that will be elucidated in the Rota decision.

"In making decisions, the tribunal of the Rota is bound, under pain of nullity, to set forth with the sentence the grounds on which it is based," said a learned doctor of the Church. "Canonists are keenly interested for two reasons, the publication of the decision in the case under discussion, which will, it is announced, appear in the next number of the Acta Apostolical Sedis. First, because it is almost, if not quite, unprecedented for a Catholic court to be asked to pass on the validity of a marriage neither party to which was, or is, a Catholic; and second, because while the plea of constraint, by force or fear, is the commonest ground of suits for nullity, it is a plea not often advanced or accepted, thirty years after the marriage ceremony. But since the Rota is a court of appeal that reviews and pronounces only on evidence, and not subjective, but objective and well-corroborated evidence, you may be sure that there is satisfactory legal proof in support of the verdict. If you knew the Rota, you would also be sure that the obvious objections of outside critics—together with dozens more that only an astute ecclesiastical lawyer could think up—have been anticipated by that insatiable heckler called the 'defender of the bond.'"

Here in Rome, indeed, where law, civil and ecclesiastical, has been a passion, a science and a fine art since the Forum was first cleared for debate, the inquirer is soon made aware that there is an immense department of jurisprudence beyond Blackstone, that this is its university and its supreme court, and that to the minds of canon lawyers the cases brought hither for judgment are primarily legal processes.

That is to say, the Roman Rota is neither a church council, nor a religious meeting, nor a pious foundation. It is a court of law, a court with a long legal tradition and a history bound up with most of the great conflicts and events that have shaken civilization. Its archives, preserved in the Vatican, are probably the most extensive and continuous court in the world. In the centuries before the Reformation it was the most important tribunal in existence, not only for ecclesiastical but for civil disputes. "Appeal to Rome" was a frequent recourse in times when the home feuds burned so brightly that judging was among the most hazardous occupations. The Rota represented then, as now, the decisions of the Holy See. It grew out of the Court of Chaplains, or auditors, chosen by the Pope to hear disputes submitted to him for judgment. Its decisions were delivered in his name. As an international tribunal sitting in Rome and composed of Judges from France, Spain, Portugal, the territory now comprising Central Europe and the different kingdoms of Italy, the Rota was, in some sort, the precursor of the present Court of International Justice. It functioned with great pomp and circumstance in stately halls in the Lateran, the Quirinal, the Vatican, or in the vast council chamber of the Palace of the Popes at Avignon, where, perhaps because there was a porphyry wheel in the center of the marble floor, or because the Judges sat in a circle and the cases were passed from one to another, or because the records were parchment rolls kept in wheel-like cases, the tribunal became known as the Rota. The sessions were opened with cavalcades and colorful ceremonial. The Judges served a strict novitiate and were invested in office with the most solemn religious ritual. They were truly magisterial, and even in the sepulture of archives their verdicts have the effect of being delivered in full canonicals.

Nothing of that ancient pomp remains in the Rota of today except the robes, or copes, of stiff purple silk faced with scarlet and the ermine collars the auditors wear on state occasions. Even its headquarters are difficult to find, hidden away at the foot of the steep street of steps climbing the Quirinal Hill. You go first to the more pretentious building next door, which turns out to be the royal stables, and are waved on by an equerry in a high hat and a flapping coat which, like the spreading masses of the King's palace above, were made for someone bigger.

The Dataria, the old palace in which the Rota has occupied a few rooms since it was reorganized by Pope Pius X in October, 1908, is all that is left to the Popes of the Quirinal. In a city where tarnished gilt and grandeur back the shabbiest enterprises, the rooms are small and unpretentious. There is a bare antechamber, a library lined with legal tomes and parchments and containing a table set with twelve portfolios, an office in which three or four clerks are not too busy, and rooms for the dean and officers of the tribunal. The court room itself is narrow and poorly furnished with a crucifix, wooden benches for the auditors, a raised desk for the presiding magistrate and a witness box, probably for the advocates. Only rows of portraits of Judges of the old Rota, some antedating the discovery of America, suggest the long perspectives of a powerful past.

Here the Rota has functioned since the "Sapienti Consilio" encyclical of Pius X, prelude to his great reform and recodification of canon law, reestablished it as one of three courts of appeal—the Penitentiaria, for cases of conscience; the Segnatura, as a supreme tribunal, and the Rota for all contentious and litigious questions referred to the Holy See for judicial investigation from any part of the world. Long before that, with the institution of the sacred congregations, corresponding to ministries or departments of government, each with its own staff and its own legislation, the ecclesiastical jurisdiction of the Rota had been greatly curtailed. It lost its status as a civil tribunal when the Popes lost their kingdom in 1870. Up to that time its decisions had the effect of laws in the Papal States. Thus shorn of authority in Church and State, the Rota turned to the other world and occupied itself in examining the claims of candidates for heaven.

Now once more an international tribunal, the court has about the same constitution as in the past. It is composed of twelve auditors, or judges, but whereas formerly these were of three classes, priests, monks and laymen, now all are priests, selected by the Pope and ranking as prelates of his household. Each auditor is assisted by a priest known as an adjutor, and both auditors and assistants must be doctors of theology and canon law. Other officers are a promoter of justice, various notaries, and, for cases dealing with marriage and religious vows, a "defensor vinculi," or defender of the bond. The court is not in continuous session, but meets on call, as frequently as is indicated by the number of appeals submitted. Its President, now Msgr. Massimi, a tireless student of the law and a theologian of great distinction, is always the dean, the oldest among the auditors in point of appointment to office. Auditors retire at 75.

Of the twelve judges, eight are at present Italians, one is Austrian, for the German-speaking peoples; one is Polish, for the Slavs, and one French. The English seat is vacant since the death of Msgr. Prior, vice rector of the Beda College, who served brilliantly for many years as dean. Another English-speaking* prelate will succeed him, but I am informed that it is easier to find a Cardinal Prefect for a congregation than a competent Judge for the Rota. Outside of Rome, where canon law is a career, good canonists are so rare that no Bishop who has one is willing to relinquish him.

The Rota may be a court of first instance, but it is ordinarily a court of appeal. Most of the cases referred to it have already been tried by diocesan tribunals. Bishop Amigo of Southwark, in whose diocese the former Duchess of Marlborough filed the petition to have her first marriage declared null, is now in Rome. Questioned in regard to the procedure in diocesan courts, he replied that in this case he appointed a special commission to examine the evidence. This is the usual custom, since only cities like Paris, which has a permanent ecclesiastical court, and Madrid, which has its own Rota, maintain regular tribunals. These special panels examine only evidence, such evidence, the Bishop emphasized, as would be considered relevant in any civil court. Contestants or appellants sometimes appear in person, but are usually represented by an advocate. In the Marlborough case the advocate was Sir Charles Russell, the distinguished English barrister, who also came to Rome. Appeal to Rome is neces-

* The Rota now has several English-speaking members.

sary, because no decision of nullity can be granted except after two concurrent decisions, one by the Rota.

Brought to Rome, complaint and defense must be put in writing or printed and copies distributed among all members of the court. These may be examined in full session, but are usually heard by three auditors only, called a "turnus," or turn of the wheel. This procedure is traditional and is followed because when the petitioners are not satisfied with the first decision they may appear again to the same court with the assurance that the hearing will be by different auditors. Thus it is evident that the Rota claims to be neither final nor infallible. It has been known to reverse itself. Ecclesiastical courts, though perhaps more cautious, have no more immunity from fraud and false witnesses than secular courts.

A marriage case is, in fact, never closed. It may always be reopened by the presentation of fresh evidence. An appeal from the verdict of the Rota may also be made to the supreme court of the Segnatura, and there remains the further recourse of an appeal to the Pope himself, who may appoint a special commission of Cardinals to review it from the beginning. It is stated on good authority in Rome that the present decision in the Marlborough case is not final. Since all the interested parties seem satisfied, however, it is hardly likely that it will drag on like the somewhat similar and equally discussed Gould-Castellane case. Count de Castellane's plea for nullity was tried three times by the Rota. The final decision was drawn up by Msgr. Prior, then Dean, and is considered by canonists a masterpiece of law and logic. It proved so invulnerable that, though the case was appealed to the Segnatura and afterward was reviewed by two different commissions of Cardinals appointed by two Popes, no loophole of escape was ever found for the persistent petitioner.

The Rota also denied the plea of the wife of Prince Rospigliosi, son of a great Roman Catholic house, in her effort to dissolve the former marriage to Mr. Parkhurst, in order to regularize her union with the Prince. In both these cases the Rota upheld the rights of Protestants against the frantic appeals of the Catholic partners, just as in its most famous case it sacrificed a kingdom, or so it boasts, rather than nullify the marriage of Henry VIII and Katherine of Aragon.

The Rota is not often advertised by a *cause célèbre*. It deals mostly with the troubles of the obscure. Of the forty-five marriage cases adjudicated by the tribunal in 1925, none was heard of outside the parishes of the litigants. Forty-five is not a large proportion of the married population of the Catholic world, and of the forty-five, thirty appeals were allowed and fifteen denied. Most of the petitions for nullity, I am informed by one of the auditors, come from France and Northern Italy and are the result of the arranged marriages of Latin tradition.* "A church that forbids divorce," he said, "must be extra careful that the marriages it enforces are real marriages, freely consented to. Consent is the essence of the sacrament. The Rota is a tribunal of recourse for young couples forced into marriage by their parents. It is not often that a plea of constraint is, or could be, I imagine, advanced by English or Americans." He added that about half the suits are *in forma pauperis,* meaning that the appellants have not means enough even to pay the legal costs of the proceedings.

Though other than marriage cases come before the court, as for instance the long-contested suit of the Augustinian Order against the Archbishop of Manila in regard to title to

---

* As of 1956, 778 cases went before the Rota; of these 256 concerned marriage and in 103 of these cases the expenses were borne by the Church.

church property in the Philippines, which the Augustinians won, it is in effect almost a matrimonial tribunal. In 1925, the marriage suits were forty-five out of fifty-four, and so far this year about the same ratio is maintained.

It was not always so. There are the files of grave and reverend seigneurs looking down upon the present sittings of the Papal auditors. There is the weight of centuries of judgment in the archives. Both conjure up endless processions of precedents. They recall the Kings who came to the Rota as anxious petitioners, the Popes who exchanged the auditor's ermine for the pontifical tiara in the days when this court was "the university of Popes" and "the nursery of Cardinals."

The official records begin only in 1171. The name Rota appears in a Papal Bull for the first time in 1418, when Martin V was Pope. But long before that the Rota flourished, and under other names the same court functioned in the veiled ages whose shadowy conflicts come to light mostly through Church councils and Papal decrees. The first thing Pope Melchiades did when the Emperor Constantine led the Church out of its underground warrens and established Peter's successor in a wing of the Lateran Palace was to set aside a hall for the hearing of contentious cases. It was called the Auditorium and witnesses that even the Christians of the catacombs were accustomed to disputation. The first auditor to cut a great figure in the world was the Roman Benedictine, St. Augustine, who became the apostle of England and the first Archbishop of Canterbury. Gregory the Great referred to him as "my auditor," and later auditors recognized him as their predecessor by placing his image on the official seal of the Rota together with that of Catharine of Alexandria, martyred on the wheel and, for her searching mind and large learning, the patron of schools of philosophy.

The layman must often be impressed or oppressed, in legal libraries and in ancient courts of justice, particularly in France, by the terrific burden of law under which the human race has struggled to its present state of disorder. But until he trails the Roman Rota through Latin chronicles and among present authorities, and learns incidentally that its history and procedure are matters which no one has ever thought it worthwhile to put into English, he never realizes how vast and comprehensive is the legal deposit of the Church and how unknown and overpowering in contrast to other codes is the body of canon law.

"Like all modern law," explained a learned ecclesiastical jurist, "canon law is based upon Roman law and the Justinian code. It is so-called because it is formulated in canons. It has, of course, grown and been modified with time and change, but it still includes the substance of the 'decretals' * of the early courts, councils and Popes expands, and when it is two thousand years old and spreads all over the globe like the Catholic Church, it naturally accumulates a tremendous deposit of law and interpretation of law. Curiously enough, only twice in the long history of the Church has this body of legislation been completely reformed and codified; once by the Spanish Dominican scholar, St. Raymond of Pennafort, under Pope Clement VIII (1592-1605), and the second time by Pope Pius X."

The recent codification of canon law, which greatly simplifies and modernizes ecclesiastical legislation, is for the most part the work of Cardinal Gasparri, the present Papal Secretary of State. Cardinal Gasparri was for many years head of

---

* Decisions of the Popes given in various forms on matters of discipline, i.e. canon law, but not always binding on the whole Church. The earliest decretals (more often called constitutions) were letters to bishops in reply to questions or reports, which had the force of law.

the Department of Canon Law in the Catholic University of Paris and is perhaps the ablest canonist in the Roman Curia. He did not lack competent assistance on the pontifical commission in a capital which contains the University of the Appollinare.

Canon lawyers from all parts of the world come to Rome for their final degrees, for though there are faculties now in most capitals, only here is it possible to study the ecclesiastical courts in operation. The Roman Congregations and permanent tribunals cover every phase of Church jurisprudence. Not the least of the functions of the Rota is to serve as a place of instruction for young canonists from the ends of the earth who may be called upon to consider tomorrow the same old scruples and contentions that have been rehearsed since the auditor Augustine was sent by Rome to make angels out of the English.

The Rota is a wheel that turns forever.

5

A NEW ROME ARISES
TO RIVAL THE OLD

January 16, 1927

A new Italy demands a new Rome. If you seek a concrete symbol of the tremendous and lively anomaly Fascism intends its kingdom and its capital to be, you have only to stand at the end of the original Main Street, on the corner of the Appian Way where once a golden milestone marked the beginning and end of all roads, and study the elaborate specifications for that booming contradiction called the New Rome. There on the slopes of the Capitol, between the forum and the tireless prancing of Marcus Aurelius, you may observe the drastic labors of young engineers and architects engaged in revising Rome just as in other offices other stern young men draw up edicts to reform and remodel the country.

One task is almost as staggering as the other. Upon a town with a metropolitan record of twenty-six centuries, in every one of which some progressive administration aspired and perspired to be eternal, enters now an ambition even more exuberant than the pagan pride that reared the biggest pleasure house in the world or the Christian fervor that built the biggest church. It wants everything, and everything at once —the catacombs and the New York subways, Romulus and Marconi, the Roman galley at the bottom of Lake Nemi and the first motor-driven leviathan on the seas.

New Rome must be the glorious evocation of the greatest capital of the past and the advance model for the greatest cities of the future. It uncovers five imperial civic centers, built by the Caesars to make room for the public business of an expanding empire, and at the same time plans a series of new civic centers on a scale that extinguishes the little enterprises of Trajan and Augustus. It tears down whole blocks of tenements in the heart of the city to reveal and parade its ruins, and with equal vigor constructs so many thousands of new buildings within and without the old walls that the boom in archaeology is only less than the boom in architecture. Except that Rome is rather less "Italian," you can walk miles in its spreading suburbs and imagine yourself in any "Mediterranean development" in Florida.

This frenzy for simultaneous exhumation and modernization is confusing. It is like a parallel-column comparison of the text of life in 26 B.C. and 1926 A.D., made to demonstrate the plagiarisms of progress. The first and last words are so often alike, and what is dug up as modern as what is newly erected. The old Rome enlarged by the new Rome's excavations bears striking resemblances, for instance, to twentieth-century America. Both go in for size and superlatives, for stock exchanges and banks, for temples of business more imposing than temples of worship. Ancient Rome not only anticipated our obsession for baths and running water, lost elsewhere for a couple of thousand years, but it invented our monotonous blocks of kitchenette apartments; it was surrounded by the country houses of tired business men. It had New York's floating population in search of amusement, and organized shows for the prodigal provincial of a magnitude that even Hollywood cannot reproduce. Like ourselves, the Romans were spectators rather than players of games. Their sport was politics and trade. The business centers shifted as rapidly as Detroit's; the five forums now being exhumed were all built on ground for which the emperors were "held up" by the owners in the best modern manner in little more than a hundred years.

The fever for building up and tearing down is not confined to the capital. The whole peninsula fumes. "Our Duomo is as worthy of a marble carpet as St. Mark's," proclaims the Governor of Milan, and the industrial metropolis is not too commercialized to wreck buildings in the most valuable business section, widen the Corso and sweep away tram lines in order to clear a great space on all sides of its pinnacled cathedral. Genoa fringes its curving bay with new docks and shipyards and becomes again the chief port of the Mediterranean and the second ship builder in Europe. Venice turns from the lagoons to the mainland to construct at Mestre a port as big as if the Bride of the Adriatic were once more the mistress of the seas. From the newly watered and revivified Mezzogiorno, or Italian Midi, Naples and Brindisi draw oil, wine and other vitamins to feed the Levant and the desert side of the Mediterranean. The longest tunnel in the

world shortens the distance between Florence and Bologna.
The longest electrified railway begins at Leghorn. New short
lines connect Milan and Rome and Rome and Naples and a
new air route joins Sicily to the mainland. Schools, roads,
aqueducts, power plants, banks and popular housing projects
multiply everywhere, while the old picture towns, from Assisi
to Ravenna, are as freshly and carefully "antiqued" as the
adzed timbers in a New England farmhouse on Long Island.

But Rome is the center of the Renaissance. And because
Rome is always in some sense the center of the world—a part
of what Mussolini calls "the patrimony of mankind"—the
fate of Rome under Fascism is important to more people
than the fate of democracy, or trades unionism, or the surplus
population. Any job of city planning, even in the young-
est and most plastic towns, is a desperate undertaking; here it
involves satisfying not only the living but the dead, and not
only the native but the critical foreigner. Nearer the million
mark today than it has ever been since the time of Augustus,
Rome was the first Italian city deprived of self-government
and put under a special régime—an imitation of the status of
Washington, it slyly assures you—in order to give the administration a free hand to compete with the golden age.

Long before the present crescendo of Romanity, modern
Rome challenged its ancestors by smothering the Capitol
under the Victor Emmanuel monument, confronting Hadri-
an's tomb with a monstrous Ministry of Justice and overshadowing Diocletian's Baths with the biggest treasury in Europe.
The three ministries being completed today, for labor, public
instruction and marine, are somewhat less in the imperial
manner, but they are scattered in different sections of the
new city, so that no part of Rome shall forget that it is a great
capital. The proclamations of the Governor are Augustan.

Even printed on the walls, which are daily plastered with more announcements than the newspapers and more exhortations than the schools, their sonorousness makes one hear again, above the shrieks of passing taxies, the voice of the prefects and the praetors.

Senator Cremonesi gets up early to cope with an office so weighted with tradition. When I mounted the endless steps of the Capitol one morning before 9 o'clock, climbing stairways walled with inscriptions of administrations beginning before the year 1, he had already been at work two hours. He showed the strain of the sixteen-hour day, but the name of Rome animated him as it animates all the tired Fascist chiefs. To him the city is the World. Never was it so magnificently dreamed of, or so carefully tended. The flowers in the public squares and gardens and in the blooming borders of promenades like the Via Veneto are changed as frequently as if Rome were Berlin or Düsseldorf. The streets are paved and clean, cleaner at their oldest and narrowest than those of any American town I know. The old stucco walls are patched and repainted in shadows ranging from cream to terra cotta. In most European capitals the height and design of buildings are fixed by the authorities; here even your color scheme is chosen for you. The idea is to preserve that effect of sunsoaked ivory as characteristic of Rome as is the sallow smoke of London, the misty pearl of Paris, the rock crystal, now so sad with soot, of New York.

The Governor introduced me to the workshop wherein his dream of the New Rome is being reduced to specifications. The chief engineer, Signor Settimi, though perched above the Tarpeian Rock and wrestling with a job that descends from the Lupercalian "beating of the bounds," is bombarded by contractors, grievance committees, Fascist ward bosses, widows and salesmen as if he were the city engineer on the less historic rock of Manhattan. He took time, however, to arrange for my instruction a sectional map of the revised and enlarged capital which no one, apparently, had ever put together before. It was like a picture puzzle, and four or five of us enjoyed the game of fitting the colored squares into their proper places. The green plots stood for parks and perspectives. All within the yellow lines was marked for demolition, mostly to widen streets or to clear "zones of respect" for antiquities. The gray margins enclosed public monuments, meaning all buildings preserved for historical or artistic reasons.

A comparison of the extent of these three zones with the total size of old Rome reveals graphically how large a part of the new plan is disinterment and exposition of the past. Signor Settimi calls his project a panoramic plan. He explains that this is the third time since 1870 that surveys and blueprints have been made for the expansion of the capital—in 1881 by Viviani, in 1909 by San Just di Teluada, and now by himself. Viviani provided for a city area of 25 kilometers, San Just for 70 kilometers, the Settimi scheme for 130 kilometers.

The latest plan incorporates and extends many of the ideas of San Just and pays the same sums, in gold lire, for property condemned and valued in 1909. The prices fixed by a condemnation committee for land expropriated today are hardly more satisfactory to the owners. The Roman city planning board has as much trouble in this respect as that of Chicago or Dayton, but it has so much more power, backed by the full force of the Government, that it proceeds blithely with its program. It starts with a government subsidy, increased by the donation of several plots of ground, the most notable being the wooded heights of Monte Mario, the commanding site destined by the American Methodists, until Mussolini got wind of their brilliant idea, for a church which should soar above and eclipse St. Peter's.

The "zones of respect" are as essential to the Settimi plan as the widened perspectives on the past are of the essence of Fascism. They are not cemeteries, but parade grounds, inciting to new glory. Yet some Romans are heard wondering whether the exposure of so many skeletons will make the old city too sepulchral. The Forum Romanum, for instance, enchanting as it is to the student, is hardly lively as a neighbor, and when to that mortuary view are added so many others— the newly excavated Forum of Augustus, the enlargement of the Forum of Trajan, the restoration of the Forum Boarium, the Theatre of Marcellus, the Augusteo and the Circus Maximus, to mention only a few of the exhumations now in process—will the past that beckons around every Roman corner become quite inanimate in its tidy and complete disinterment?

Certainly it must lose some charm of contrast and confusion. In the Middle Ages ancient Rome was spent too freely; the present passion for the antique saves it too carefully. The buccaneering builders of the Renaissance were grand and flamboyant at the expense of the Caesars. They made Rome a chronological crazy-quilt, of writhing façades masking barnlike old basilicas, of baroque palaces flaunting classic marbles and haphazard columns, of satiric fountains spraying Egyptian obelisks and Roman baths. The patchwork was not beautiful, perhaps, but it was alive, and as intemperately and robustly Roman as the Forum and Colosseum must have been in their gilded and grandiloquent prime.

Rome always borrowed, stole, used and Romanized whatever it wanted. One likes the Theatre of Marcellus with a
charming palace built in its arena and congeries of slummy
shops burrowing under its dark arches. It is exciting to find
a modern Stock Exchange hiding behind the grave columns
of the Temple of Neptune. The sight of the Mussolini Cabinet at mass in the church Michelangelo fashioned under the
arches of Diocletian links Fascism with the two great Roman
Renaissances. Dining on summer nights in a little garden res-
taurant scooped out of ruins, one felt nearer to Trajan than
one does in the cleared apse of the Basilica Ulpia that replaces it. More interesting for its vandalism is the Papal chan-
cery constructed of travertine from the Colosseum. Rome
seems eternal and indestructible less in the mournful impressiveness of neatly roped-off ruins than in living walls made of
fragments of dead epochs or today's roofs supported by the
pillars of yesterday.

On the other hand, since the chief business of Rome is government, antiquities and sightseeing, archaeological areas are
probably more profitable than commercial buildings. A city
of consumers, without manufactures, trade or international
banking, it has nothing to keep it going and growing but
State employees, ecclesiastical students and tourists. Its prod-
ucts are only edicts, dogmas and glamour, and if a million
people can be supported by such "imponderables," to use
one of Mussolini's favorite values, then the Settimi plan of
showing off the ruins represents the best possible investment
of Roman real estate. Rome's gold mine is history. No other
city can raze a tenement and uncover all the strata of civilization. Romans must live; and perhaps they live most comfort-
ably by moving out to the suburbs and leaving to the rest

of us the thrilling relics of a wall as Tarquin built it, of a city as Caesar knew it, of a house as Claudia planned it, and of a life so long buried that it is as fresh as yesterday's.

In justice to the Fascist project it must be added that there are red and white as well as green and gray and yellow zones on the new plan. The white indicates the buildings that stand, all the modern city and every shred of the old of all epochs of any account worthy of preservation. The red represents new construction, and it would give a false idea of the whole scheme not to say that the red on the map is not more striking than the astonishing magnitude of the actual building operations.

I have seen Florida at the boom, Athens mushrooming to house Smyrna and the refugees, Bucharest doubling its population after the war, Louvain and Arras and the crumbled towns of Flanders beginning over again, but never anywhere so much construction at one time as now proceeds in and around Rome. Other Italian towns grow visibly and volubly. The too-sudden industrializing of an agricultural country tends to abnormal urbanization. Rome expands because Italy is in the ascendant, and in consequence of the unprecedented centralization of government, which cuts down bureaucracy in the provinces but concentrates an army of employees in the capital to take care of the municipal, communal and labor administration of the entire country.

Circle the Aurelian Wall, until now always too big for the city it enclosed, and you will see whole new towns of apartment houses, trading centers and suburban villas. They stretch south toward Frascati; westward along the electric railway to the sea and Rome's new bathing beach at Ostia; east along the Via Nomentana to the "Garden City" whose

narrow little houses and American front yards perch like a
mechanical toy town on Monte Sacro; north enclosing the
Flaminian Way and across the Tiber to the newly plotted and
developing slopes of Monte Mario. In addition vast banks,
insurance offices, hotels and warehouses replace the worst
tenements in the old city or rise on the site of monastery gardens and villas in the Ludovisi quarter.

City planners from richer countries are always impressed
by the originality and especially by the gayety of the new
Italian substitutes for the slum. A New York architect, in Europe to study housing schemes, says he has found nothing
better over here than the Roman workers' suburbs.

In the workshop on the Campidoglio wherein Rome is being officially refashioned, the architects and engineers are absorbed in other problems. They are opening up perspectives,
planning civic centers, working out the traffic tangle, poring
over restorations. They burn with the Roman ardors of Mussolini and Cremonesi.

Further in the future are a subway and the elimination of
all tram and horse traffic in the central area, a hundred more
fountains added to the three hundred now splashing in every
square, a "university city" to make Rome an international
center of secular as well as ecclesiastical studies. It is impossible even to keep on enumerating here all the impatient projects crowding towards realization. Enough is suggested to
show that Rome rises, that in three years it has gone further
than in fifty.

6

PIUS XI AND MUSSOLINI

June 14, 1931

Just ten years ago, in June, 1921, two citizens of Milan might easily have passed each other in the Rome railway station. Coming and going, they might have been sprayed at the same moment by that fountain in the Piazza dei Termini, which suggests to the traveler one aspect of the eternity of this city that started as a forum: from a hundred mouths the waters rush like the roar of eternal controversy, or eternal laughter. Whatever befalls the railways, the fountain never stops. Those were the days when the Italian trains were not on time, but the two passengers from the North were hurried fast enough to keep their appointments with destiny. In the Vatican Pope Benedict XV, holding his last Consistory, was bestowing upon Msgr. Achille Ratti the red hat which marked him as eligible to the Papacy. On Montecitorio King Victor Emmanuel, opening the last Parliament of democratic Italy, presided at the political debut of Deputy Benito Mussolini.

Nobody connected the two events. In the next year the new Cardinal was the head of the Church and the new deputy was the head of the government, but few then foresaw that they were elected to solve the long-festering, "insoluble" Roman question, last obstacle, it was said, to the union of Italy. Still less was it foreseen that the settlement would lead to a new debate between Church and State, in which the Pope would contend for the rights of the individual and the Premier would affirm the infallibility of the State.

Yet the atmosphere of Rome was sultry during those June days. An air of suspense like a moral sirocco hung over Italy. As in the world today, everybody felt the approach of change and scanned the horizon for signs and portents. To an American seeing for the first time the ceremony in the Hall of the Consistory, the pageant itself was eye-filling enough to erase the troubled present.

There was silence as the new Cardinals filed in, but one, and only one, was greeted by a burst of cheers, surprising in that place and quickly suppressed. The man thus singled out walked with a quick step; his small, alert eyes seemed to twinkle behind thick spectacles; he had the brow of a thinker and the tight lips and firm chin of a man of action. He would have been distinguished in any company by his expression of serenity; even there he looked pre-eminently the priest— calm, self-possessed, remote from the tensions of the hour. "That," volunteered the Englishman, standing in front of me, "is the Archbishop of Milan, a great scholar and very popular here as former director of the Vatican Library. I wonder what sort of Pope a librarian would make? Tenacious, this one, I fancy; slightly Wilsonian."

The Archbishop of Milan and the editor of the *Popolo d'Italia* may have met in the two years during which Mussolini mobilized his "Bundles of Fight" and the churchman, returned from his mission of regularizing the relations of Church and State in the new Poland, presided over his native diocese, the most highly industrialized and then the most restless province in Italy. At least once they confronted each other in the Duomo square—at the funeral of the twenty victims of a Communist bomb which exploded in the Diana Theatre in March, 1921. The Archbishop in his black vestments blessed the dead from the steps of his pinnacled cathedral while Mussolini, in black shirt, stood at the head of the first Fascist legion.

During the ceremony priest and Fascist may have had thoughts in common. The Papal Nuncio in Warsaw was the only diplomat who remained at his post when the Bolsheviki marched to the gates of the city in 1920. As "Russian Visitor" for the Holy See he had traveled along the vague borders of the Soviet empire in the hungriest and most chaotic days of the revolution. He had negotiated with the Kremlin for the release of imprisoned priests and Bishops. What he saw made him dread the first signs of the same revolution in Italy—the red flag flying over labor headquarters and city halls, the daily "annoyance strikes" disorganizing public services, the preliminary skirmishes of class war. Long before that, moreover, when assistant in the Ambrosian Library to one of the most distinguished Oriental scholars of his time, Msgr. Ratti developed a keen interest in Eastern problems and Eastern religions. Intensifying his repeated protests against religious persecution in Russia is a life-long concern in the fate of the Orthodox Church.

If they met in Milan, there is no record of any interview between the Pope and Premier in Rome. Though their careers have run curiously parallel and their public conversations have been heard around the world, so far as any one knows they have never talked together. The pontificate of Pius XI began in the same year as the Fascist régime. But it was several months before the march on Rome that Pius took a tentative but significant step in a new direction; he was the first of the "prisoner Popes" to appear in the outer loggia of St. Peter's to bless the Roman crowd. Mussolini, for his part, hearing that as head of the Vatican Library Msgr. Ratti had tried to purchase the historic Chigi library, collected by a Chigi Pope, made the graceful gesture of presenting it as a gift from the Fascist Government to the librarian Pontiff. The new ruler preached religion, restored the crucifix to the schools, went to church at the head of his Cabinet, and made instruction in Christian doctrine an integral part of the Fascist educational system.

It was evident to all that the way was being paved toward reconciliation. The Popes knew that Rome was irrevocably the capital of Italy. There was nothing they wanted less than to govern it or be burdened with a papal kingdom. What they wished was independence, a foothold on the earth that belonged to no other sovereign. With a stroke of the pen, at the last moment, Pius struck out of the settlement the proposed cession of the grounds of the Villa Paphily-Doria. What he accepted, in the 160-acre Vatican City, was practically the extraterritorial space allowed by the rejected law of guarantees, the difference being that it is now set apart by bilateral treaty, an agreement between sovereigns, instead of by grant of Italian law. What Mussolini gained was prestige, a brilliant diplomatic victory, the enthusiastic support of the majority of the Italian people. He remembered the words of Crispi:

"The greatest Italian statesman will be the one who will solve the Roman question."

Probably he was too realistic to expect also peace and collaboration. The Pope did not wait for territorial independence to raise his voice against the Fascist claim of State supremacy. As prisoner in the Vatican, he took the liberty of issuing "dissenting opinions" free, he multiplies encyclicals, sets up a super-power radio station to reach the ear of Italy and the world, and publishes in season and out of season uncompromising Catholic doctrine on every controverted subject, from birth control to socialism. Particularly, or so it must seem to Mussolini, he makes occasions to dispute the Fascist theory that the citizen exists for the State and must be so educated. In his own person, indeed, the Pontiff whose picture has been put in the State school books has come to be something like the voice of the Opposition in Italy.

On both sides, and no doubt recognized by both sides, were large reservations to complete agreement. The negotiations that culminated in the Lateran Treaty* of 1929 lasted nearly three years. The accompanying concordat, which is not part of the treaty proper and might therefore be separately abrogated, was painfully worked out and is in some respects the most favorable to the Church ever signed by a modern State. Hundreds of conferences took place, at which, as has been noted, the two chief negotiators never met. Afterward the Pope received the King and his family for the first time since the usurping House of Savoy took possession of the old Papal Palace of the Quirinal. There was no audience for Mussolini.

---

* The solution of the Roman Question. By this the Vatican yielded to Italy many former territorial rights and received in return nominal compensation. The Lateran Treaty established the relationship between the Italian State and the Church, and the City of the Vatican thereby became a permanently neutral and inviolable territory. It is called Lateran because it was consummated at the Palace of the Lateran attached to the oldest basilica in Rome.

Pius XI has conversed with President Hoover, while both were engaged in relief work in Eastern Europe, but not with the Premier of Italy. And since the Popes grant but do not issue invitations to audiences, the inference is that the Fascist chief has not asked to be received.

Despite official accord, the two powers in Rome could hardly meet except in debate. Between the domains of God and Caesar, everywhere and always, there is a wide border-land of disputed territory; but between the conception of the State developed by fascism and the claims of any Church there is real contradiction. This becomes more apparent as time goes on. One notices in Rome today a new wariness in the attitude of churchmen toward statesmen, and vice versa. Both seem to be on the lookout for danger signals. This fundamental opposition does not, however, diminish the general satisfaction in the achievement of the Lateran treaty. When the Pope referred to Mussolini as "a man sent by Providence" he meant it, meant that here was the instrument, appearing at the opportune moment and endowed not only with the will but with the power to end the historic deadlock between Vatican and Quirinal. Without such concentration of power in one man, the question might easily have remained open another fifty years.

Divergence of view was inevitable, expected, in a sense reassuring. Neither signatory could have acquiesced in having the treaty regarded as an alliance; either in the international field, where for seventy years the policy of Italy and the Vatican has been to preserve their independence one of the other, or nationally, considering how many elements in the Fascist party derive from the anti-clerical groups of the past and how many elements in the Church were once affiliated with the old democratic parties. Mussolini understood this, also that the sole power of the Pope is the power to protest, the eternal *non possumus;* all the police power resides in the hands of the government. So the debate went on, the only debate permitted in the oldest forum.

Then suddenly the police power was invoked. Little attention would have been paid to the Vatican's protest against excesses of Young Fascist zeal in raids on Young Catholic clubs—incidents as collegiate as scraps between rival schools —if it had not been followed by a summary government order closing 15,000 Catholic clubs. That action proved the friction deeper and more general than any one had suspected.

The charge, scoffed at in Vatican City, is "political activity." It recalls to me a street fight I witnessed in Rome ten years ago, an engagement in the hot feud between Fascists and members of the Popular party. The founder of the "Popolari," the exiled priest, Don Sturzo, was also at one time the executive secretary of the Federation of Catholic Societies, known as the Catholic Action, against which the present police measures have been taken. Don Sturzo was a social reformer, organizer of the White Federation of Labor, and the labor program of the Catholic party was too radical for a good many conservative Catholics. It was formulated in part, though it went further, on the encyclical, *Rerum Novarum,* of Leo XIII, the pronouncement reaffirmed in the recent encyclical of Pius XI on the relations of capital and labor.

The Pope praised the ideal of class collaboration underlying the corporative State of the Fascists, but suggested that the system might be improved and that it was the right and duty of Catholic associations to work for Christian solutions of economic problems. When it is noted that the first attack on the Catholic Action appeared in Lavoro Fascista, organ of the Fascist labor corporations, it becomes clear that this utterance of the Pope, linked up with memories of old political contests, aroused resentment and suspicion. It goes without saying that any organization is a possible political nucleus in Italy today, just as in the modern social complex it is almost impossible to prevent any activity from becoming somehow and somewhere "political."

The labor corporations are integral parts of the Fascist State. So also are all the curricular and extracurricular activities of the youth of the nation. And the fundamental contest is here, in the struggle for the mind and soul of the child. The purpose of creating a Fascist generation is as single-mindedly pursued in Italy as is the development of a Soviet generation in Russia. Both systems adopt the methods of the Catholic Church, the one to make militant Fascists without God, and the other to make militant Fascists with God—but according to the Fascist formula rather than that of the Church. "Ah, youth!" exclaimed Mussolini when I spoke of spending an afternoon at the headquarters of the Balilla. "There you see our Italy. There we are strong, heroic, a new race."

He was right; he might have added that in this breed of young Fascists he has his nation, 2,000,000 eager, ardent and as far as possible faithful copies of Mussolini. But the training of youth is also the chief concern of the Church. There is a disputed territory far more important than that covered by the Lateran treaty.

The controversy in Rome is always described in the headlines as between the Pope and Mussolini and the designation aptly describes a distinction. Though so little alike, the disputants have characteristics in common; both are fighters, preachers, workers. The Pope is twenty-five years older, but at 74 he works as hard, hits as hard, receives ten times as many people. In him the "inflexible" meets the inflexible, if you get the difference; the "intractable" encounters the "intransigeant." But he has to speak, not in his own person, but as the Pope. His personality is submerged in his office. He is only one in the 1900-year-old line of Pontiffs whose names are mostly forgotten, whose awful duty is to act as "vicars of Christ on earth." From generation to generation they reiterate the "eternal verities" of their faith.

The wonder is that their inhuman eminence does not completely depersonalize the occupants of the See of Peter. Actually they differ sharply in character and method, and no three men more than the last three Popes. All Italians, of course, all from the North, Venetian, Genoese and Lombard, they are as distinct as the three epochs, pre-war, war and post-war, of their reigns. Pius X was the peasant elevated to the Papacy. He impressed by his goodness and simplicity and retained toward the world to the end the attitude of a parish priest toward his parish. He was among the first casualties of the war that turned his parish into a shambles. Benedict XV was the patrician and the diplomat, whose unprepossessing exterior had so much vividness, curiosity, irony and sagacity. He was peculiarly fitted to steer the difficult course of the Church through the war years; some one has said that the diplomatic victory in the war was the Vatican's. It was the only court in Europe that came out of the struggle with enhanced prestige.

Pius XI came from the middle class, the son of a small-town merchant. He had had brief experience in parochial work, teaching, diplomacy, but he was chiefly known, when elected Pope, as a learned librarian with a record for Alpine climbing. Later, perhaps because he was more desirous than his predecessors of settling the Rome question, it began to be said in Rome that his special fitness was to deal with Mussolini. At first he slowed up even the measured pace of Vatican procedure, insisting on going into details, reviewing documents himself, examining his own witnesses. He took a long time to come to decisions; it was soon observed, however, that they were decisive. His mind was that of a research worker, and once he had mastered his material he set about installing modern machinery, as far as possible, to deal with it. As director of one of the world's great centers of research, Monsignor Ratti was noted among students of all countries for his labors in making its inexhaustible archives accessible and easily usuable. He installed the latest systems of cataloguing and classifying, called upon the resources of science to restore old manuscripts, employed every modern device to preserve and display ancient and fading codices.

His method as librarian is typical of his policy as Pope. He has furnished the Vatican offices with the most up-to-date equipment. While the mellow old rooms look as they always did and not a relic of the past has been disturbed, the Empire State Building has not a better telephone system or more efficient files. No Pontiff has used so many inventions of science or used them more consistently in the service of religious dogma and ancient law. He is, in a word, the Pope, and thus proscribed by the precedents, the traditions, the overwhelming pretensions of his ministry, he has to carry the past into the future. Vigorous as is his character as a man, wide as is his knowledge as a scholar, he does not speak on his own authority.

He is, nevertheless, under compulsion to speak. In this sense he is not so free as Mussolini. The head of the Fascist State is under no compulsions save those he has created for himself. He is the government. Pius is not the Church, but Mussolini is this new State he has called into being. He directs its evolution, formulates its philosophy as he goes along, chooses his traditions and makes his own precedents. That is not to say that he escapes the hard compulsions of economic necessity, national necessity, the supreme necessity of holding together the fractious elements of the Fascist party. But so far his personality has been stronger than his militia. He is the one dictator more powerful than the dictatorship. If the régime has tired Italy, Mussolini never has; to greater effect than any living statesman he has exerted personal magnetism. Thus the idea of a supremacy of the State over the individual gains its greatest vitality in Italy from this emotional and persuasive, this purely individual force.

In the remarkable speech he made to the Senate in submitting the Lateran treaties the Premier interpreted the agreement in terms immediately protested by the Pope. Such unequivocal language was necessary, said the Duce, in order that no one should imagine that the effect of the accord would be to "Vaticanize Italy" or "Italianize the Vatican." He predicted that causes of friction between the two sovereignties would inevitably arise but that the peace itself would be lasting because it represented a historical and practical necessity. This may be taken for granted, for when the controversy of today is fairly studied, it will be seen that it has little to do with the old Roman question.

But the new Roman question which it raises is far older and more difficult to solve. It is the ancient dilemma of tribute to Caesar and the tribute to God, complicating as the functions of the modern State invade all the territory once held private. The Pope claims that the citizen is first a man, Mussolini that the man is first a citizen. No conflict is as fundamental as this, and seldom has it been waged with such dramatic simplicity as now, in the Pontifical city, between rulers who symbolize spiritual and temporal power, at their most uncompromising.

7

VATICAN DISTURBED
BY GENEVA MOVES

October 15, 1935

In Vatican City the developments in Geneva are regarded with misgivings and as heading toward general war.

Missionaries who have been received in private audiences in recent days found Pope Pius XI intensely preoccupied with events and saddened by the daily worsening of the outlook.

Three times since the Papal Secretary of State inaugurated the three-day prayer for peace in the Catholic world at Lourdes last July, the Pope has prayed for peace with direct references to the Italo-Ethiopian conflict.

Late in August, while addressing an international congress of nurses, he expounded the doctrine of the church in regard to aggressive war. A month later he denounced the crime of war, particularly war of conquest, to 15,000 war veterans gathered in Rome. The third time, it is learned on good authority, he spoke to Mussolini himself.

What the Pope said to Il Duce will never be known. In his public utterances the Pontiff confined himself to enunciating the moral law that an act of unprovoked aggression is never justified. On both occasions, however, he warned against action that would aggravate and enlarge the danger of war and referred to the moral and social necessity of finding peaceful means of satisfying legitimate needs for national expansion.

Pope Pius plainly warned statesmen of the world that it is not enough to abhor war, to pray for peace or outlaw aggressors. They are bound to deal with the causes of conflict, he said.

Every day the Pope receives hundreds of letters from all countries begging him to intervene in the African imbroglio. This mail is opened by four secretaries in his presence. Much of it he reads himself. Indeed, it is learned he is engaged in glancing through a pile of letters from England.

Some letters are sent to him as "Dear Pope." One writer, an officer in the British Army, told him he ought to resign unless he could stop Mussolini. The invariable rule of the Holy See is not to reply to criticisms or communications on controversial questions.

As head of a universal church whose members fight under all flags, the Pope maintains strict neutrality in secular disputes. His duty is to formulate general moral principles to make clear the doctrines and positions of the church. If he condemned a specific nation or a specific war, it is explained in ecclesiastical circles, he would put unjust blame upon hundreds of thousands of young men, like the soldiers in the Italian Army, who act in good faith and obey their government out of the highest patriotic motives.

8

THE POPE STEERS A COURSE
AMID STORMS

December 15, 1935

Pope Pius XI assisted recently at the memorial mass celebrated annually in the Sistine Chapel for the Cardinals who
have died during the year. Around him that morning were
grouped most of the living Cardinals of the Curia. Beyond
the lovely marble screen of Mino da Fiesole they sat in two
rows facing one another, their bent white heads and crimson
capes overshadowed by Michelangelo's "Last Judgment"—in
a world of dark signs perhaps still the greatest handwriting on
the wall. The Pope himself sat apart, on a throne beside the
altar, a hieratic figure that nothing overshadowed. In his stiff,
bell-like cope, his tall miter, he looked rigid and symbolic
as the rock of Peter.

At public functions Pius XI has this quality of immobility

that makes every one around him appear fidgety and nervous. His vigor is extraordinary for a man of 78. His strong-featured face is still bronzed after a summer spent at his villa on the terraced hills above Lake Albano. His black hair is only sprinkled with gray. As he intones the benediction his voice is firm and resonant. His step is heavier but as decisive as on the June day in 1921 when he entered the nearby Hall of the Consistory to receive the red hat.

Even more extraordinary than the Pope's vigor is his quietness. It is not the quiet of serenity; there is too much iron in it for that. In the Vatican they speak of him as "a born Pope," meaning that his character is as papal as his office. In a period so overwhelmed by shouting rulers, he is the only one I have seen who suggests force in repose.

Those who know the Sistine Chapel remember it for the splendor of its frescoes. There the greatest artists of the Renaissance outpainted one another in the procession of masterpieces running like a frieze around the side walls. From the ceiling Michelangelo's prophets and sybils brood over the ineluctable mystery of man; and on the end wall he left that blackened judgment and revelation which must have startled his time as much as the indictments of Rivera shock ours. To recall in that place the murals of the Detroit Museum, of Dartmouth College, of the just-opened Aula Magna of Rome's new University City, is to wonder if the moderns of today will remain after 400 years as timely, or as timeless as these.

Really to see the Sistine frescoes, however, they must be seen as the back-drop of the pageant for which they were painted. When the officers of the mass move before the altar, when the Supreme Pontiff and the princes of the church, the Swiss Guard, the papal chamberlains, files of clerics in purple

and scarlet, people the choir, then the sober-colored walls and
the scene below become part of one picture, blurred alike by
incense and the sense of crowding centuries. And really to
hear the Sistine Choir one must listen to the disembodied
voices issuing from the little gallery and filling like one ineffable voice the space for which the choir was created.

But though choral and spectacle help, they do not of themselves produce the atmosphere which struck one observer
most that morning. I had hardly realized how tense and
troubled and super-heated is the air of Rome when suddenly,
here in the heart of Mussolini's straining capital, I found my-
self in a place where everything was slow and calm. It was
not peace exactly—this strange relaxation. If any spot is
seismological, sensitive to every spiritual tremor that shakes
the earth, it is the Vatican. It was not detachment, for the
Holy See, and particularly its present occupant, is intensely
interested in the events and movements of the time. After a
time one perceived that it was perspective; mounting the
Scala Region out of St. Peter's Square, out of the Rome of
sanctions and militant resistance, one passed out of the short
into the long view of things.

Everything presses on the Vatican that presses anywhere,
but the very walls repeat that everything passes, too. Mussolini must do what he has planned to do this year, this hour,
so he believes, or it will be forever too late. Combinations
alter so quickly that no political ruler today can count on tomorrow. In the Vatican there is not only all the time there
is, but a kind of continuum which makes the interval called
Now both longer and less important than it is in the Fascist
era, the Roosevelt administration, the life of a British Government.

The reigning Pontiff is the 260th of his line. Beholding him surrounded by the old Cardinals who will choose his successor, one saw not only that the Holy Father himself is always venerable but that he is an old man elected by old men. Most Popes are well over 60 before they begin their pontificates; Pius XI was 65 when he assumed office in 1922, the year the Fascists marched on Rome. The See of Peter will never be stormed by a youth movement, and there is something oddly steadying even in that hierarchical fact—at least, if you have traveled over Europe surveying the effects of youth movements and revaluing the ripeness and tolerance of age as a guarantee against the violent reaction of adolescence.

Individually the Pope is seasoned by a lifetime of priestly experience before he becomes chief pastor of his world-wide flock; officially he is one link in a lengthy chain. The attitude toward current problems of the most contemporary of pontiffs is thus in a sense non-contemporary. He comes from further back in time and looks further ahead than other rulers. His authority and responsibility are of an order so different that even when he pronounces on the same questions he speaks with another accent and another purpose.

This contrast between the secular and ecclesiastical measure was perceptible to the dullest observer present on successive days at the celebration of the Italian Armistice Day at the Altar of the Country and at this memorial service in the Sistine Chapel. At one commemoration, seventeen years ago was "the dead past"; at the other, time merges into eternity; a hundred years are reckoned as a day.

That is a truth to remember first in interpreting papal policies. They change and evolve with the times more rapidly than any one would guess who has not followed the story of the Holy See since 1870, a comparatively brief interval; but the mind of the church never loses the perspective of an old institution which has survived a good many world upheavals by refusing to be stampeded by any passing crisis.

Nothing illustrates this point more clearly than the stand of the present Pope on the raging question of competence and power of international law to preserve peace by punishing the aggressor. From all over the world, day after day, in public exhortations and private appeals, Pius XI is passionately urged to intervene in the conflict that has broken out at the very doors of the Vatican.

The Archbishop of Canterbury and the prelates of the Church of England have been especially insistent on the Pope's duty as the head of the Catholic Church to condemn Italy for wantonly breaking the peace. The least the Bishop of Rome should do, declare the most zealous, is to uphold the efforts of the League of Nations by invoking against the invader nation the powerful spiritual sanction of the church —the sentence of excommunication.

Now it is evident that peace is a paramount interest of a universal church as truly as it is the essential interest of the British Empire, which all Britons consciously or unconsciously serve. And for somewhat similar reasons. It is fact that the outbreak of the World War literally broke the heart of Pius X, because of threatened disaster in terms of spiritual empire, also—cutting communications, interrupting normal life, crippling missions, upsetting the whole existing order. More, a universal war, in which worshipers at the same altar slaughtered one another, was a kind of indictment of a universal church. Beyond the human tragedy stalked the moral failure represented by this reversion to the law of the jungle.

The war was over when Pius XI became the Keeper of the Keys, but his pontificate has covered a period of social and spiritual turbulence almost darker than the war years. From the beginning, recognizing how strained and fragile was the armistice in which the exhausted nations lived, his chief preoccupation has been to widen the bases of peace. Years before the present crisis developed the Pope warned the statesmen of the world that their policies were heading straight for war.

During these years the Holy See itself has been immersed in a many-sided struggle. Benedict XV played the ungrateful rôle of neutral between two battle lines; the present Pontiff has had to steer the ancient bark of Peter through whirling cross-currents of change and revolution. He has seen the collapse of a great established church in Russia, and was the first to recognize that the essential significance of the Soviet experiments is as much religious as social.

He has watched a ferocious persecution of the Catholic Church in Mexico and the now cohering fight for independence on the part of all religious confessions in Germany. He has frequently crossed swords with Mussolini in a long and successful campaign against the extreme claims of fascism in Italy. From the viewpoint of a dogmatic church, no more dangerous heresy has ever arisen than the arrogant assumptions of the totalitarian State, whether it is with God, without God or against God, to paraphrase a famous dictum.

Pius XI is intensely interested in the events and movements of his time. He reads widely, catechizes all his visitors, dips into thousands of letters. You would not believe how many people write directly to the Pope if you did not see the baskets of letters carried into his study every morning. Still less would you imagine the scope and character of these epistles.

Obviously, it occurs to people of all persuasions, all over the world, to confide to the Supreme Pontiff their family difficulties, their spiritual problems, their material needs. As many advise him what to do as ask his advice. A large proportion ask for money. The Pope does not answer these letters personally, but on hundreds he draws a line in red pencil opposite the main point of the letter and sends it off to be dealt with by his Nuncio in the country whence it comes or the Bishop of some distant diocese.

A recent visitor found him with a pile of letters from England on one hand, a book describing the new political tendencies of France on the other, and in front of him *The London Times,* which he reads every morning. After a perfunctory inquiry as to the visitor's health—and Pius XI has little concern for the ills of the flesh, in himself or others—he plunged without preliminaries into a keen discussion of world affairs.

In character he is not so much austere as habitually serious. He seldom smiles or relaxes. His thoroughness and tirelessness are proverbial at the Vatican. He knows the dioceses under his charge as well as he knew the books on his shelves, when he was librarian of two of the great libraries of Italy. He has organized the administration of his handkerchief-size kingdom to the last detail with the most businesslike precision.

The Vatican has been completely modernized during his reign, and many of its great art collections have been rehoused. He has built enormously, for use rather than beauty, in the space at his disposal since Vatican City became the smallest independent State in the world. It is due to him that it is so small; he deliberately cut out of the final settlement the adjoining Villa Doria and its park which Mussolini wished to cede. "The Church wants independence," he said, "not territory."

"Everything this Pope touches he tidies up," remarked an old monsignore rather somberly, and you can see his passion for order and system in the arrangements of Vatican City and in the model dairy farm he has constructed at his country villa at Castel Gandolfo, where the scrubbed "papal briefs," as the dairymen call the newest calves, swagger in blue-tiled stalls that are the marvel of the countryside.

Stronger still is his passion for order in the world. Political order, social order, moral order. The Pope is terribly anxious as he looks out upon the gloomy confusion of the secular scene. Through his thick spectacles the policies of contemporary statesmen seem above all discordant and short-sighted, concentrated only on the immediate.

In the effort to chart a Christian course for the social revolution, he resurrected and brought up to date a famous encyclical of Leo XIII, *Rerum Novarum,* and embodied its principles in his own encyclical, *Quadragesimo Anno.* Last year the sociologists seeking to reform the Swiss Confederation were studying this document. The late Chancellor Dollfuss drew on it in planning the Austrian Guild State he did not live to inaugurate. Father Coughlin* asserts that he found there the inspiration for his Union for Social Justice.

Above everything Pius XI has worked for peace. In 1933, seeing the thickening clouds on the horizon, he proclaimed a "Holy Year," inviting to Rome the faithful of all nations to form a spiritual union for peace. Ever since his every public utterance has been an appeal and a warning. Before the Italian military concentration in Africa became war— supposing it is war—the Pope spoke out strongly on at least

* Father Charles E. Coughlin, Pastor at Royal Oak, Michigan, was at the time a radio orator on social and economic problems.

three occasions, condemning unprovoked aggression as a crime against the moral law.

Referring to the Italian argument that the war was justifiable as a defense of frontiers against incessant dangers, and necessary for the expansion of a population increasing day by day, the Pontiff declared it should and must be possible to reach a solution of such difficulties by means which do not involve war.

"One thing seems to us certain," he concluded. "If the need of expansion is a fact of which account must be taken, the right of defense itself has certain limits which must be observed if defense is not to become guilty. In any case we pray to God that He may second the activities and the efforts of men of clear vision who understand the exigencies of the true happiness of the peoples and of social justice; that He may bless the efforts of all who do their best, not by means of threats, which do nothing but irritate the spirit and aggravate the situation, rendering it every day more difficult for those who work for pacification with the sincere intention of avoiding war."

Since the war began the Pope has made every effort to bring hostilities to an end. He has had, it is reported, one of his few interviews with Premier Mussolini, whom Pius XI never met until after the accord settling the Roman Question was signed. It would be interesting to know what took place at this meeting, for both Pope and Duce are men of iron will, used to command, equally direct and forthright, equally sure they are right.

There is no doubt they understood each other; the head of the church does not mince words with the head of the Fascist State. And Mussolini has shown himself wiser than Hitler in avoiding unnecessary clashes on the home front. His attitude toward the church is conciliatory. Recently, in reply to a sharp protest from the Pope when the civil authorities decreed work on Sunday to make up for Fascist holidays during the week, the government immediately rescinded the order.

For the first time since 1870 the Pope has the status of a temporal sovereign; for the first time in sixty years relations are normal between the Italian Government and the Holy See. Many think the international position of the Vatican is not so strong with the Pope as a sovereign in an enclosed State as it was when he was the "prisoner" of Italy. Against that view must be placed the improved status of the church inside Italy; the greater freedom of the Holy See, which not only controls its own communications system but publishes the one uncensored newspaper in Italy; and now, at the first test of war, its complete immunity from the operation of sanctions.

Nevertheless, sanctions make a problem for the Vatican as well as for the Italian State. You can't function in the midst of a blockade and remain untouched by its restrictions. But it is not for that reason that the Pope takes the gravest view of the League measures to stop war. It is because sanctions are war—and one form of war leads inevitably to another.

The single thought of the Vatican is not preventive war but peace. Pius XI has not been asked to intervene in the conflict, but it is no secret that he is doing his utmost, unofficially, to speed the work of conciliation. The chance to come to terms before the application of sanctions was lost, but the Holy Father has repeatedly declared that the situation seems to him so full of danger that no responsible authority dare miss any opportunity of using influence to avert catastrophe.

Why, then, one asks, has the "peace Pope" not condemned Italy? Why has he not fulminated directly against this war? Why has he not used his moral authority to back the stand of the League of Nations against the aggressor nation? Because, say theologians, the province of the Holy See is to enunciate the moral law but not to apply it in specific secular disputes. For one who might blame the Pope for not intervening in a "moral issue," thousands would criticize him for interfering in what to them is a "political issue." His mission is to teach, to interpret the doctrine of the church; he does not pass judgment in conflicts of national interests, even when one side affronts the conscience of the world.

It happens that Pope Pius is on peculiarly friendly terms with the three principal parties in the present dispute. He has been twice to England on missions and is known to have a special tenderness for the country and the people, as well as a real respect for the British Government. Since the war, for the first time since Henry VIII, the British Government has a Minister to the Papal Court, sent at the direct instance of the King. Despite its inevitable clashes with the Fascist régime, the Vatican owes to Mussolini the historic reconciliation which put an end to an abnormal estrangement between church and State and is perhaps the most important of all factors in uniting a long-divided country.

Add to this the special interest the present Pontiff takes in the Ethiopians. The only college within the confines of Vatican City has been built for students from Ethiopia, forty of whom now study in peace and safety in the heart of the enemy country, under the direct protection of the Pope. Pius XI has been on cordial terms with the Negus ever since, as Ras Tafari, the present Emperor of Ethiopia visited the Vatican ten years ago.

Thus personal predilections, the Pope's duty as head of an international communion, and the policy of the Holy See combine to prevent Pius XI from taking sides in this dispute. There is something more. Every utterance of Pius XI proves to the attentive reader that in the perspective of the Vatican the moral issue does not appear so simple as it does to members, say, of the League of Nations Union. Freely interpreted, it is clear that Pope Pius holds that judgment cannot be passed on one set of facts without weighing all the facts.

Italy is clearly wrong in her method of seizing by force what she needs, he seems to say; but what right means has the society of nations devised to deal with a problem like Italy's? Birth control, it goes without saying, would not seem a moral solution to the Pope; and even if the population remained static the Italian peninsula cannot support 44,000,000 people or even contain them without an explosion somewhere.

The League unquestionably is right in taking action against a breaker of the covenant; but is it right in making its first strong stand on the punitive side, enforcing Article XVI* while ignoring Article XIX, which provides for revision of treaties and correction of injustices? Moreover, in defending the weak against the strong with one hand, is the other using the peace principle as an instrument to preserve great powers in their possessions? As to Ethiopia, whose moral rightness on all counts no one has questioned, the issue doesn't seem to be too clear. As the empire disin-

* Article XVI provided sanctions for any member of the League resorting to war in disregard to its Covenants, and described steps to be taken by members of the League against a member going to war, e.g. economic sanctions. Italy attacked Ethiopia in October, 1935; both countries were members of the League.

tegrates before the invaders' walk-in, how much of it can be called an independent nation?

In a fog of moral issues, a tribune of morals might well hesitate to pick out one sin for punishment. No thoughtful observer in the world today can define the uneasy peace we labor to save as a just, even a possible peace. It is a peace established by war and designed to keep the world forever as the war left it.

This peace is itself so hideous a proof of the futility of armed conflict that it explains the dread and hatred of war and war-makers sweeping over the world. Nothing better or more stable can be established by more war, that is certain; but in the long view it is equally certain that there must be war—not all the sanctions in the world can stop it—until there is a league not to enforce but to create peace by working for a true equipoise, political and economic, and giving all nations instead of a favored few a vested interest in the status quo. If the Pope condemned, where would the condemnation fall?

9

FOR STATE OR — CHURCH?

March 1, 1936

At the crack of dawn any Sunday morning in Germany you are likely to be wakened by the tramp of Hitler Youth starting out on one of their patriotic excursions. Or maidens in uniform, sturdy and firm-footed, gather under your window to go places. These early outbursts of "strength through joy" soon merge in more traditional sights and sounds, however, and by the time the mellow bells begin to chime and the churchgoers appear, well-brushed, dutiful, a little more self-conscious than of old, the clean and quiet streets resume the familiar Sunday aspect. The German Sunday still retains an atmosphere more sabbatical than Sunday anywhere, even in England. It restores the effect of continuity you lose on weekdays as you watch one Germany moving toward another in a series of sudden jerks, backward and forward, like a train driven from both ends.

Germans easily form congregations. They are the church-going people par excellence. Something like 90 per cent of the population—as many as vote "yes" in a Hitler plebiscite —are inscribed as church members. More than half of this membership is merely nominal, but the fact that it is voluntary, and entails payment of the special tax by which religion is supported, argues a tenacious habit of allegiance to the church. A large but dwindling proportion of German children, perhaps 40 per cent, attend Confessional schools, Protestant or Catholic, and even the so-called communal, or State, schools provide religious instruction, imparted at stated hours by ministers of the various denominations.

The church is important. Germans do not love old forms and establishments for their own sake as the English do, but they cannot live without order and observance, expressed in institutions, systems and—up to now—in sects.

Protestantism has a special power and authority in the land of Luther. It is organized and integrated into the life of the people to a degree unknown in other countries. Catholicism, too, is strongly rooted, not only in provinces predominantly Catholic, like Bavaria and the Rhineland, but in Prussia itself. The Catholic Church has been fortified by repeated struggles and distinctly shaped by the character of its environment. You see that in the Italian Tyrol. If there were no other sign that Bolzano is still Boetzen, for instance, you would know that the cathedral is a German church.

Religion is important. Nowhere is revelation taken more seriously than where biblical criticism developed into a scientific method, almost a scientific passion. Skepticism itself is fervent in Germany. It tends invariably to form schools, even creeds, of doubt. "You have to think and care a lot about religion to be a heretic," an old French abbé once said to me, and the intensity of feeling on both sides of the conflict agitating the Reich at this moment proves that the issues involved appear as vital from one point of view as the other.

Not that the German struggle is either the classic contest between church and State or a war against religion as such, like the anti-God campaign of the Bolsheviks. The National Socialist invasion of the religious field is in part the attempt to subjugate the ecclesiastical or the zeal to supplant Christianity by a folk religion, "the German faith movement," more suited to the German soul, is the new conception of the State itself as God. This brings an element into the situation never encountered before in quite the same form, and therefore never tested.

In Italy the authoritarian State means really the authority of one man, which has limits, both in scope and time, and does, after all, leave certain fields untouched. The dictatorship in Russia is the most all-pervasive the world has known, but it is fundamentally the dictatorship of a theory, already greatly modified in practice.

Like its models, the Third Reich is that latest form of absolutism, the party-State; but whereas communism has universal aims and fascism is aggressively nationalist, neither system presumes to base policy, law, religion and economics on the idea that the State is a race, or the race a State, with all exclusiveness and inclusiveness implicit in that extraordinary notion. Totalitarianism in Germany differs from the wide pretensions of similar régimes by going deeper; in addition to the blank ballot it requires also a blood test as a proof of conformity. The nation is conceived as a "blood brotherhood."

To understand the proportions and implications of the church conflict, one must realize that the driving idea of the Hitler government is to make Germany one at all costs. The unity aimed at allows for no differences, local, political, ideological, spiritual.

The national ideal, as the Fuehrer declared on the third anniversary of his accession to power, is "one people, one spirit, one will, one energy," to be achieved by a training which will make "every German a sincere and effective National Socialist." There must be an end of sects, say those entrusted with this training; they cannot see why the process of unification should not develop one church, a truly national church, in which Catholics and Protestants would be happily incorporated.

One must realize further that this ideal unity does not yet envelop the governing group. The rulers of Germany are anything but of one mind in the religious dispute or any other controversy. If confusion of thought and a crisis of conscience stir under the surface order and cohesion the régime has achieved, it is because so many contradictory voices are shouting directions. On one side the attempt to make the church subservient not only to the State but to the philosophy of the State is made in the name of Christianity. "The church Germany wants is not a State church," says Dr. Kerrl, Minister for Church Affairs, "but an inwardly free, absolutely independent church, which nevertheless through its new conception would quite voluntarily march with the State in which it must work and live." And then he adds the watchword of this march: "If order is to be es-

tablished, only one order can exist"—an order based on the
organization which the State sets up.

On the other side, there is the strange *Weltanschauung*
outlook on life more and more impressed on the nation, and
constantly on the young, in the name of National Socialism
itself. This trumpets into patriotic dogma the thesis of Professor William Hauer of Tuebingen University, that the
Teutonic race does not develop naturally, to its full force
and stature, under the Christian "philosophy of submission."

Professor Hauer and Count Reventlow, the original pro-
moters of the German Faith Movement—a Nordic religion
distinct from Christianity—are now overshadowed by official
prophets like Dr. Alfred Rosenberg, the importance of whose
anti-Christian crusade springs from the fact that he is the
chief editor of Herr Hitler's paper, the *Voelkischer Boe-
bachter,* and carries the resounding title of "Commissioner
of the Fuehrer for the Supervision, Instruction and Education of the Whole National Socialist Movement."

Lest there should be any doubt of the validity of Dr.
Rosenberg's commission, the official leader of the Reich
Youth Movement, Baldur von Schirach, goes up and down
the land preaching the same ideas. So does Herr Himmler,
head of the secret police and leader of the Nazi élite, the
SS. When to these voices are added the broadcasts in the
same tenor of Minister of the Interior Frick and Minister
of Education Rust, not to mention the caustic contempt for
the churches expressed on occasion by Minister of Propaganda Goebbels, it becomes clear that if one lobe of the
official brain works to "regulate" the churches for their own
good, the other is intent on sweeping them into the discard.

Meantime people of all confessions are in a state of deep-
ening bewilderment and dismay. Government spokesmen are

inclined to dismiss the whole church agitation as "political." "No order or unity has existed in the Evangelical churches since the beginning of the republic, when the old relationship with the State was broken," one official informed me. "When Hitler came to power they all welcomed a proposal to unite under a single administration. Ever since there has been dissension among the leaders as to what form this administration should take. But don't forget that the dissension covers a good deal of opposition to the régime. Members of old political parties use the church squabbles as a sort of last stand to work up feeling against the government.

"With the Catholics it is a different matter. The priests are making a fight for the education and control of the young. We hold that this is absolutely the province of the State, particularly against an organization under international authority, like the church of Rome. And there is no doubt that in Catholic resistance we are meeting what is left of the spent force of the once powerful Center party."

"Political?" reply the denominational leaders in accents varying from honest perplexity to despair. "But what is non-political and what is to be left as the province of the church? Is the church mixing in politics when it protests because the State fixes conditions for the administration of the Christian sacraments—baptism and marriage—and now proposes to order the divorce for political reasons of properly married couples?

"Can the Christian church surrender the right to preach the divine law because new codes base justice on principles never before held valid? We are told to confine ourselves to the religious field when our fight has no other object but to save some field for religion, to guard the church from becoming a mere subdepartment of government."

Dr. Niemoeller, the former submarine commander who is the leader in Berlin of the Confessional movement in the Evangelical church, had the temerity to issue in January a pamphlet, immediately confiscated, in which he said that a State church in Germany means something quite different from a State church in other countries.

There he touched the crux of the conflict in the Reich, for here a State church means a church of the National Socialist State with its totalitarian claims—"an instrument of the political authorities," he wrote, "instead of an instrument for the preaching of the Gospel according to the faith of the fathers without respect of persons."

"In this respect at least," sighed a worried pastor, "the Jews are better off than the Christians. Nobody wants to unify or coordinate the Jews, so they are left alone in one place—the synagogue. Their children are practically forced into Jewish schools, while pressure of all kinds is brought to bear on our children to draw them out of the denominational schools.

"I know parents who lost jobs because their children attend religious schools. Other parents unwillingly withdraw their children from our schools because attendance fatally handicaps the young in the fierce competition for work. The irresistible pressure is on, and from the children themselves. They want nothing more than to conform, to be in step. You can imagine what it means to a child in present-day Germany not to belong to the Hitler Youth—to stay at home while all the boys and girls march off for Saturday sports or Sunday excursions. You can imagine, too, what happens when they do belong and what religion they inevitably imbibe."

The school registrations tell the story. Observe that in Munich, the most Catholic city in the Reich, in the recent enrollment for next year the number opting for the lay schools is 35,000 and for the Catholic schools 19,000. Last year the figures were exactly reversed, 19,000 for the secular and 35,000 for the parish schools, and at that time the church authorities were concerned because the number had dropped 15 per cent compared with the year before.

The present remarkable turnover followed a vigorous campaign, in which the National Socialists held more than thirty public meetings, while prohibiting any opposing propaganda. All sorts of threats were employed to deter parents from being so unpatriotic, so un-German, as to choose Confessional schools for their children. The Nazis celebrate the result of their drive as a great victory for "unity," as indeed it is. It proved not only that the ruling party is determined to abolish church schools but that it is succeeding.

Are the churches, then, fighting a losing battle? It is too soon to approximate an answer to this large question, which goes far beyond the immediate issue. Nor can an outside observer pretend to measure forces Germans themselves have no means of evaluating. In this new sum called totalitarianism—meaning that two and two and ten times two always make one—it is very difficult to "weight" your figures justly; too many immense calculations have to be made by guesswork.

But certain facts are pertinent and suggestive. The first is that after three years of tremendous, though uneven, pressure the churches are the only organizations in Germany that stand out publicly for independence. The great political parties dissolved without a struggle. The trades unions were easily absorbed in the Labor Front. Proud military associations like the Stahlhelm surrendered. Even the Brown Shirts are gradually diminished and reduced. All secular opposition is silenced, but ecclesiastical resistance to coordination and absorption is louder today than it was in the beginning.

The second fact is that despite the force of the tide sweeping the rising generation from its old religious moorings, church attendance has increased. Everybody remarks it, and the visitor can see the enlarged congregations for himself if he takes the trouble to look in at church services on his travels. One reason is that the church has become a sort of assembly hall, since meetings of church societies cannot be held elsewhere and the pulpit, now the sole place where the pastor can communicate with his flock, is interesting as a news center. "The chancel is the only place where we can enlighten the public," declared Cardinal Faulhaber in the pastoral letter read in the Munich churches before the school "plebiscite," "for public meetings and printed propaganda are denied us."

It is not surprising to find the high-naved, gray old Dom of Munich packed to the doors for one of these manifestos of its fighting Archbishop, or to see crowds from distant parts of Berlin filling the suburban church of the fearless Pastor Niemoeller. But it is impressive to come upon full churches nearly everywhere and to breathe in all the same atmosphere of tension, as if the congregations were consciously holding the line against an attack which astonishes as much as it perturbs.

Both Protestant and Catholic opposition is on similar grounds. Dr. Niemoeller opposes the Nazification of the Evangelical church. He charges that the administrators set up by the government, from Bishop Mueller to Dr. Kerrl, operate to make the Protestant church a minister to the new worship of the State. The real aim of the authorities, he says, is manifest in the propaganda among the Hitler Youth and in the exit from the church of large numbers of those who represent the mind of the régime, like members of the SS, the picked Hitler guard.

More than one Bishop of the Confessional movement has defied the new church law promulgated in December, on the ground that obedience implied a complete surrender of episcopal functions; and more than one has been warned by the church section of the secret police that he was laying himself open to charges of high treason.

The Catholic fight centers particularly on the youth organizations and the Confessional schools. The Catholic church stands on firmer legal ground than the Protestant, because its relations with the State are governed by a concordat with the Vatican, an international instrument signed by Herr Hitler himself in 1933. This does not save them from what they claim to be violations of this treaty, however, nor the clergy from a long series of arrests, some for indiscretions in the pulpit, others on charges of smuggling money out of the country.

The wide publicity given these trials and the heavy punishments inflicted on the offenders, guilty of paying debts by methods formerly encouraged among German businessmen, is one way of embarrassing the church and weakening its influence. But though the Vatican has let the law take its course and has not protested against the arrest of so prominent an ecclesiastic as Dr. Bannash,, vicar-general of the Berlin Diocese, for the "treasonable" offense of conducting a church information service, it notes every breach of the concordat and there is no likelihood that the well-knit Catholic organization will budge from its position.

The third point worth noting is the effect on the régime itself of spreading dissension and disquiet among those sections of the population naturally disposed to be its strongest support. To be fair, it must be said that large numbers of Germans accept the government's program for an all-embracing national church. I have heard mothers complain that their sons and daughters will be alienated from the church unless the religious bodies go along with the national movement.

In the beginning the good-will of all the Evangelical groups was so great that the majority responded gladly to the summons to unite under a single administration. They chose as Reich Bishop the universally respected Dr. Bodelschwing, but this saintly and eminent churchman lacked the proper National Socialist zeal and he was soon supplanted by Dr. Mueller, an army chaplain, who was an old friend of the Fuehrer's. Through Dr. Mueller the party was able to assert itself—and to split the uniting front in three, with the acquiescent "German Christians" at one end and the fighting independents of the Confessional movement at the other.

Then began the struggle against dictatorship in the church, which has been developing ever since toward a crisis. The clumsy and shifting policies of Bishop Mueller made way for the laissez faire administration of his legal counselor, Dr. Jaeger. Finally, after two years of successive tightening and loosening up of ultimatums, truces and general confusion, a Minister for Church Affairs, with dictatorial powers, was appointed in the person of Herr Hanns Kerrl.

During the five months of Dr. Kerrl's strenuous campaign to organize the church on the party pattern, the struggle has sharpened and deepened. Resistance of the militant Christians of all persuasions has stiffened as church ordinances are promulgated by the State as if they were civil laws. Many others are indifferent. Almost all the young are heart and soul with a movement they are taught to think of as a religious revolution.

But any one scratching the surface must see that the soul of the nation is troubled and divided. It is not too much to say that the church contest—not only because the church is important but because the issue is clear enough to throw light on much else that is obscure—is the central conflict in the Reich today. It has spread opposition to the régime in wide areas where no opposition existed.

Why? What strange impulse drives a government to create unnecessary enemies by proceeding in one whirl of combat against Jews, Protestants and Catholics all at once? Why alienate its best citizens? Suppose the effort should succeed; by weakening the hold of the churches, by devitalizing the Christian tradition, is not National Socialism undermining the solid, stable base on which its own power rests?

The answers lie in the new phenomenon of the insatiable State, which lives by consuming everything, sees in every contrary opinion a threat to itself and loses all sense of measure or limit. It is doubtful if a free church can exist in such a State or, if it can, whether it is not bound, by its very assertion of religious liberty, to curb the secular power. In Germany we see the first real engagement between the organized church and the totalitarian State. In Russia the revolution liquidated the Orthodox church as an institution. In Italy there is practically only one church, and the State, after a few tussles, left it supreme in its own province. The National Socialist State aims both at subduing and preserving the church, and by penal law at imposing a racial religion. The church says "No," and no affirmation in the confused chorus of the Reich sounds quite so positive as that reluctant negative.

10

PIUS XI AT EIGHTY

May 31, 1937

The Pope is 80 years old today. He began his pontificate at 65, the retirement age under the Social Security Act but a fairly young start for a Pope, a ruler chosen out of an electoral college whose members seldom become Cardinals until they are pretty venerable. For this reason, the Pontiffs of the Catholic Church are usually old men whose terms are short. But at 65 Cardinal Ratti was not an old man. He was a robust, black-haired, athletic prelate, born in a mountain village in Lombardy, who had spent most of his working years in the quiet of research libraries and all his vacations in the quiet of the most inaccessible Alpine peaks. Up to a year ago he showed few signs of age: his hair was still black, his step firm, and his unabated vigor wore out his secretaries. Until last November he had never known illness himself or borne it patiently in others. "The will is stronger than the body," he used to chide his enfeebled juniors.

Strength of will is the dominant characteristic of Pius XI. Around the Vatican they speak of him as "the rock" against which nothing prevails. Undoubtedly his will has kept him alive this year and driven him to excessive efforts to meet challenges as shattering as any the Holy See has had to face in its long and troubled history.

His eightieth birthday is signalized by a blast from beyond the Rhine which presages a war against the church carried on with all the resources of police power, propaganda and economic pressure. It strikes the octogenarian with special force, because if the iron will of the Pontiff was ever over-ruled, it is hinted in Rome, it was when he renewed the concordat with Germany in 1933, after Hitler came to power. In a recent encyclical letter* to German Catholics he admits that he signed this agreement with misgivings.

The Papacy is the oldest existing dynasty. Its annals cover nineteen centuries of history, mostly a history of struggle, and it may well be that the present Pope will stand out in the record because his reign coincided with the birth of fascism and the realization of communism. It happens that he ascended the papal throne in 1922, the year Mussolini assumed power in Italy, and this coincidence largely determined the character of his pontificate.

Of all the paradoxes of a time sown as thickly with paradox as with propaganda, none is more striking than the development in the shadow of St. Peter's Dome of the most exaggerated "etatism" in history, a conception of the state which

* Known under the title, *"Mit Brennender Sorge."*

would not only crush but supplant the church. The early ages of the Christian era were filled with the struggles of the church to exert its spiritual and often its temporal authority over secular governments. Then came the struggle, not yet over in many countries, for separation of the two powers, the attempt to strike the balance in rendering unto Caesar and unto God.

For fifteen years, as fascism evolved and spread, Pope Pius XI and Mussolini have confronted each other across the narrow, tawny waters of the Tiber, two sovereigns of opposing kingdoms who share the same capital. They are linked by the Bridge of the Angels, and that isn't far from what's left of the arches of the bridge Horatius once defended. Perhaps it is because their capital is filled with such aids to perspective that they have been able to sign a treaty to respect each other's zone of authority. In a predominantly Catholic country this agreement works fairly well so far. Even so, it is a contingent truce, negotiated and observed with reservations. Unguarded as it is, the Tiber is a frontier, and a closely watched frontier, at that.

The Lateran treaty is eight years old. Unless all signs fail, the agreement the Pope concluded with Hitler, already broken in fact, will not last half as long even in form. Yet signs often do fail when policies depend on the impulses and hunches of one man. Europe has been shaken time and again in recent years by sudden and unpredictable unilateral decisions, and these affect internal as well as external affairs. Observe how the emphasis veers even now in Germany from the anti-Communist campaign to this attack on the Catholic Church, directed precisely where it will do most damage to the moral prestige of priests and teachers, and precisely where church authorities have been concentrating their own fire—on conditions in Nazi schools and camps.

In any event, the worn old Pontiff cannot end his days in peace. His villa on the shores of Lake Albano has gardens overlooking the Roman campagna. Equipment and methods in the Vatican have changed more in his tenure than in a hundred years before. What Castel Gandolfo mostly signifies, however, is that the Pope is no longer "the prisoner of the Vatican." Yet this new freedom is disturbed by pilgrims from Germany, pilgrims from Spain, voices from Right and Left, all telling the same story of repression and persecution. It is not a happy birthday for a Pope who loves order and peace.

11

THE NEW POPE

March 3, 1939

One thing certain about the new Pope* is that he will follow closely in the footsteps of his predecessors. As the Papal Secretary of State, Eugenio Cardinal Pacelli had admiration amounting to veneration not only for the person but the policy of his chief. In a recent conversation he said that Pius XI felt obliged to raise his voice on every possible occasion in the defense of liberty of conscience and the inalienable rights of the individual soul.

Pope Pius felt he had to speak, the Cardinal repeated with so much force, that it was clear that the Pope's chief adviser felt the same sense of obligation, adding in effect, that "where if not here could the voice of Christendom be raised?"

A fortnight before the death of Pius XI this correspondent was received by the Cardinal Secretary of State in his scarlet and gold offices in the Vatican. The appointment was for 11:30 o'clock. On the dot he appeared in the reception room and on the stroke of 12 he rose from the sofa on which he

* Pius XII was elected on March 1, 1939.

sat and walked with the visitor to the door. This punctuality impressed because it was rare in the interviewer's experience with secular statesmen.

His personality is even more impressive than his precision. No member of the Sacred College so perfectly looks the part of a prince of the church. His tall, slender figure has remarkable dignity. His face is thin and ascetic, with long features and deepset, questioning eyes.

He has the manner of a great gentleman, simple, modest and assured. He speaks English clearly and well. His expression is much more lively than the photographs indicate. In Rome he has the reputation of being austere, even cold, so it was rather a surprise to find him smiling, warm and vivacious.

Perhaps this was because his condescension touched on two of his great enthusiasms. One was the Pope. The almost boyish fervor with which the new Pius spoke of Pius XI and of his heroic fight against the "terrible heresies of the times" is the best clue to his own conception of the papal office.

It was soon after the British Prime Minister had visited the Vatican. The Secretary of State did not dwell on the impression the British statesman made on the Pope, but he waxed eloquent on the profound effect the Pope's words had on Mr. Chamberlain. There was then no question of the Pope's death, and when the visitor remarked in some connection that in the United States the Cardinal was known and considered *papabile*,* he brushed aside the suggestion with as much impatience as his perfect courtesy would allow him to show.

---

* An Italian expression meaning an eligible and likely candidate as successor to the Papal throne.

His second enthusiasm was for the United States. He spoke of his airplane flight across the great American Continent and of the largeness of the view, the tolerance, the free atmosphere of America. Evidently the freedom struck him most. No other atmosphere, he implied, was so conducive to the free practice and free growth of religion.

Most of the half hour's conversation was devoted to the church's foreign policy. It was not an interview, so the Cardinal who is now Pope cannot be quoted. He discussed gravely and frankly the pressing problems of the Vatican today. Obviously he is a deeply spiritual man whose wide experience as an ecclesiastical diplomat has not abated his zeal or his piety.

He is particularly and personally interested in the situation of the church in Germany. He mentioned that he had spent ten years of his life as Nuncio in Berlin, negotiated two concordats and learned to have an immense respect for the spirit and firmness of the German Catholic hierarchy.

It is no mere expression to record that in the view of the new Pope the church has no foreign policy except to defend, where attacked, the vital interests of religion. Formal governments are no concern of the Vatican today save as they interfere with the right of the church to care for fundamental human rights.

No one who has talked with Pius XII can doubt that on that point he will be as uncompromising as the Pope whose name he has assumed. He is a diplomat where Pius XI was primarily a teacher. He is of a different temperament and different training and his methods may not be the same as those of his predecessor, but he is swayed by the same ideas and the same view of duty of a Pope in the modern world.

12

VATICAN MOVE MAY BE A SIGN
DANZIG TALKS ARE NEAR

May 29, 1939

For several weeks Pope Pius XII has been sounding out the principal governments of Europe in an effort to find a basis for a reasonable discussion of the international disputes that threaten war. He has instructed the Papal Nuncios accredited to the various capitals to invite the interested governments to consider "with peaceful intentions" the solution of the grave issues disturbing the world. He has suggested to each either a meeting of all the nations concerned in these disputes or a series of bilateral talks to thresh out particular questions.

It is characteristic of the mind and method of the present Pontiff that his first avenue of approach to these problems is through diplomatic channels. And it is characteristic of the temper of the times that so far his tactfully phrased inquiries have met little response. By training and lifelong experience, Pius XII is a diplomat. In the secular diplomatic service he would be called a career man. The prelate he chose to succeed him as Secretary of State, his closest associate in the direction of a vast international organization, is also a career diplomat, Cardinal Maglione, former Nuncio to Paris. The most astute of British diplomats recently told the writer that in forty years of diplomatic service he had never met a more accomplished diplomat than Cardinal Maglione.

But the Pope is more than a diplomat representing, as he says with his rather wistful smile, "only the kingdom of heaven." He is a spiritual plenipotentiary of great influence, though he has none but moral weapons to impress a world at arms. This correspondent has had the privilege of two conversations with Pius XII in recent months. The first was when he was Secretary of State, shortly before the death of the former Pope. The second was about three or four weeks ago, and already the burden of the Papacy lay heavy on his slim shoulders. He was erect, alert, interested and questioning as before. If anything, his manner was simpler and humbler and his keen eyes more gentle. But he looked paler, thinner, more troubled.

For more than twenty minutes Pope Pius talked so easily, sitting at his crowded desk in the long, crimson-walled library where he works, that the listener could have forgotten his high office if it had not been implicit in the extraordinary contrast between his view of the world and that of other rulers and statesmen interviewed across the Tiber, across the Alps, across the ocean. Never as now, when everything is so instant and urgent, was it so apparent that the Vatican has a different measure of time. At the end of a long round of capitals preoccupied by questions of prestige, military computations, political bargains, physical danger, it was like coming into another dimension to see the whole scale of values reversed, and the whole scale of forces, so that it didn't seem to matter where were the most guns or the greatest armies. The Pope spoke as casually and confidently of "the help of God" as the French speak of the Maginot Line or the Germans of the "150,000,000" iron men, wherever they are, behind the Axis.

He spoke of his peace efforts. It was not long after the dispatch of President Roosevelt's letter to the dictators, and he referred to it with greater sympathy than was evinced in most high quarters in Europe. Whether there was any connection between that move and the diplomatic initiative of the Holy See in support of settlement by discussion, it is certain that one followed closely on the heels of the other. The Vatican based its private but more general plea on the same ground as the President. It did not make specific appeal to two governments only, but it insisted, like the President, that, "for moral reasons based on the well-being of humanity," every means should be exhausted to avoid the terrible ordeal of a war which would be more homicidal than that of 1914. It is interesting that the appeal circulated by the papal envoys several weeks ago has just been made public. Does this indicate that the Vatican has received hints that it is opportune to bring forward the idea of discussion of grievances? Mussolini repeated at Turin that the immediate questions before Europe, obviously Danzig and the Italian claims against France, were not worth a war. There is some reason to believe that the first exchanges—very unofficial, very tentative—are being made on the latter issue. Are the Poles or the Germans ready to talk about Danzig?

The questions are suggested not so much by the Pope's effort as by the possibility that the establishment of a new balance in Europe has increased for the moment the risk of other tactics and encouraged a turn toward negotiations. There is no doubt that the Pope would be quick to take advantage of such a turn. He is a man who feels deeply, as his predecessor did, that he has tremendous spiritual responsibility not only to his own flock but to the world. He has dedicated his pontificate to the search for peace. It is clear to any one to whom he speaks that he is driven by the sense that as Pope he must do something to save the human race from the awful catastrophe of war. It is clear that he believes, not that war is the worst of all evils, but that it will bring social and moral chaos in its train, disastrous to all he is commissioned to defend.

13

MYRON TAYLOR
AND THE VATICAN

September 26, 1942

The visit of Mr. Myron Taylor to the Vatican underlines in a striking manner one great advantage accruing to the Holy See from the Lateran Treaty. We are so accustomed to the paradoxical and the unprecedented in this war that hardly a ripple is stirred by the extraordinary fact that an envoy of the President of the United States has traveled through enemy territory with the permission and under the safe conduct of the Italian Government and for more than a week has been engaged in important conferences in Vatican City.

Actually, therefore, Mr. Taylor is freely expounding the American point of view within the physical confines of an enemy capital almost within sight of the gloom-filled palace

where Mussolini sits. This could not have occurred during
the last war, supposing Italy had then been on the other side.
It is the result of the guarantees given to the diplomatic envoys to the Holy See under the terms of the treaty signed by
Mussolini himself, and shows how this agreement, while it
cannot give full independence to a purely nominal and undefended state like Vatican City, does improve the political and
diplomatic position of the Papacy in relation to other governments.

This importance is further attested by Mr. Taylor's mission. Before the Roman Question was settled, the Popes con-
tended that in time of war they could not communicate freely
with the outside world while the Vatican was part of the
kingdom of Italy. By an odd twist of history, it has remained
for a country without official representation to the Holy See
to make the first international test of the Lateran Treaty.

The Lateran Treaty works to our advantage as well as that
of the Holy See. We may be sure that the President would
not have sent a representative to confer with the Pope unless
he considered the visit highly useful. And such a visit in the
present circumstances would be impossible unless the Vatican
on its pinpoint of territory had the status of an independent
state, and a neutral state.

This consideration should dispose of the idea that Mr. Taylor's purpose is to urge the Pope to take sides in the war, a
conjecture as far-fetched on its face as the guess that His Holiness proposed the visit with the thought of trying out some
sort of peace feeler. The President is too realistic to imagine
that the head of a Church with millions of adherents in both
camps can do more than exert strong moral influence on the
side where the interests of Christianity lie, and Pius XII is
too well informed to misunderstand either the position of the

American Government or the firm determination of the American people to fight this war until it is won. Perhaps no statesman was more anxious that the stand and intention of the United States should be made unequivocally clear to all concerned from the very beginning of hostilities.

The obvious explanations of Mr. Taylor's mission are the most logical ones. It may be assumed that his primary purpose is to acquaint the Vatican with the views and aims of America at war. The fact that the visit was under discussion for many weeks in Washington suggests that the initiative came from here.

More and more as it develops, the struggle becomes a spiritual as well as a military and political contest. All the freedoms we defend are the extension of the fundamental human right of free will, a right which is at once the basis of natural law and of Christian philosophy. Hitler's conquests in Europe have served to demonstrate beyond any doubt that the survival of the Church is linked up with the survival of the principle of democracy. The lesson is by now so clear that in all the occupied countries the most open and defiant opposition to Nazi tyranny comes from the religious leaders. This is strikingly true in Germany itself. It is creating a new situation in Spain. The moral prestige of Marshal Petain is undermined by the mounting resistance of French Bishops and clergy to Vichy's surrender to German pressure notably expressed in resistance to the deportation of refugee Jews.

Vatican City is a center of spiritual power. Physically isolated as it is in enemy territory, it is important that those who direct its policy should not be out of touch with American ideas and plans. The unusual length and number of Mr. Taylor's interviews with the Pope and his advisers are an indication of their eagerness to be informed.

Undoubtedly peace was discussed in these long exchanges —not "a" peace such as the Axis may propose before the tide turns against it, but the peace that will be made when the war is won. The shape of this peace is the Pope's chief concern. No secular ruler is more interested in the restoration of normal law and order or in the kind of world organization that will follow the war. His five-point peace plan is thought in the Vatican to be in harmony with the aims expressed in the Atlantic Charter, but an enormous number of moral and religious problems are involved in the working out of these plans.

There are many good reasons for exchanges of ideas between the White House and the Vatican as the war develops, but the chief is the urgent need to secure the cooperation of all the moral forces for the winning of the war. Mr. Taylor's mission may be interpreted as a move in the wide field of moral strategy.

14

THE BOMBING OF THE
CAPITAL OF CHRISTENDOM

July 21, 1943

The bombing of Rome shakes the Western World because it brings home with a special poignancy the schism within our civilization which is at the root of this war. At last our bombs have fallen on the triune and many-layered city that is in some way ancestral to all who share the great heritage of Western law and culture. They were aimed with most meticulous accuracy to separate the Fascist city and its malignant war growths from the older Romes—the capital of Christendom and the monumental city—literally the Eternal City—that preserves in living stone a unique record of our common civic history.

The tragedy of Rome is that the three cities huddled together beside the Tiber cannot be completely separated. A careful circle can be drawn around St. Peter's and the Vatican, but only a miracle could save the basilica of San Lorenzo Outside the Walls when the adjacent freight yards were struck. The old walls would fall by concussion if not by direct hit. The capital of Christendom is not only the tiny neutral state called Vatican City, headquarters of the Catholic Church. It is Rome itself, the Rome of the catacombs, of St. Paul's and St. Clement's, mother of all the Christian churches. Only Mecca for the Mohammedan world, or Jerusalem, cradle of three great faiths, has anything like the religious significance of the Eternal City.

The tragedy of Rome is that Fascism sits as a usurper in the capital of Christendom. The trail of fire and ruin left by the bombers leads back to the March on Rome. This was the first manifestation of heresy of the twentieth century, and as we look back we see that it was not by chance alone that the worship of the State set up its altar in the central see of a universal church, or that it chose the Forum, where the ancient tribes came down from the hills to debate for the scene of a new tyranny which stifled all debate.

There is as much reason to bomb this city as any other war capital. It was long ago taken over by the enemy of the civilization it typifies. Its religious and historic character was used as a shield and a shelter for the warmakers. Yet civilized man can derive no satisfaction from the destruction of cities anywhere, and even though he accepts the miltary necessity of bombing Rome as a communication center, he is peculiarly troubled in this case because Fascism is so recent an interloper on a stage peopled with overpowering memories. He is confused when he perceives that to save civilization he is destroying places and things always associated with civilization.

In other words, the tragedy of Rome, where the dividing line cannot be exactly traced between what we want to keep and what we want to smash, reflects in a measure the tragedy of our time. Monday's deadly raids, the most carefully planned and precisely carried out in the history of air warfare, reemphasize more strikingly than ever that we are waging two wars at once, a political and a military war. There is no possible way of divorcing one from the other. The strategists realized the political and moral risks involved in the bombing, as is evident in the clear warning contained in the President's assurance to the Pope that Vatican property would be respected, in the detailed explanation issued when the raid started, in the presence of civilian reporters in the bombers to verify that the instructions were carried out to the letter.

Rome was not bombed to demonstrate that it could be done. Italians knew this already; the raids on Ostia and the near-by airfields had already demonstrated to the capital that we are supreme in the skies over Italy. It was not bombed to force capitulation; the people know this is inevitable eventually. The only question is when. Therefore the main objectives must have been, first, to save time by cutting off supplies for a delaying action in southern Italy; second, to tell Italians in unmistakable language that they cannot be safe anywhere, and, third, to convince them that the Germans are less dangerous enemies, commanding less power of destruction, than the Allies.

Some questions left by the raid only the future can answer. The political risks were greater than the military. We shall soon see whether they were justified. Was it, as emphasized in the British press, an all-American enterprise, and if so, why? Will it leave a residuum of bitterness in non-Fascist Italy and in other parts of the world that will carry into the post-war period?

Herbert Matthews,* in his graphic and conscientious account of the bombings ended with the remark that "history like justice, is blind." The blind are the history makers, unable to see the final effects of their own acts. The blind are those who set this conflict in motion. The scene was Italy, in 1921, and if in 1943 we are all caught up in the terrible train of events, the grueling conflicts, growing out of that challenge, so that at last we have to bomb cities and destroy the heirlooms mankind has treasured for centuries, it is because we cannot kill the disease without hurting ourselves. We cannot free the holy places where the wreckers have dug themselves in without damaging the outer walls.

* Herbert Matthews, New York Times Staff Correspondent.

15

THE NEW MARCH
ON ROME

June 3, 1944

Millions of people who have never seen the Eternal City are seeing it today through the eager, straining eyes of the doughboys who have fought their way through the slitlike lanes of Velletri and climbed beyond it to a spur of the Alban hills which looks down on the rolling Campagna to the Dome rising like a shimmering bubble out of the jumble of tawny-colored roofs and towers and lesser domes that cover the Seven Hills—the history-weighted hills that are themselves so small.

This is the characteristic view of Rome from the south. One minute the peacetime traveler along the Appian Way is at the foot of the mountain wall. The next minute the slopes drop behind and he gazes, as from a top gallery seat, through curtains of old trees, olive, cypress and stone pine, at the Roman plain, set like a stage with the landmarks of history, filled with stones that already forget Mussolini and his march on Rome and remember "old, far-off, forgotten things and battles long ago." They will not forget the present march.

The soldier from the beachhead has waited a long time to see that changeless view. It has taken him not a few minutes but days of bitter struggle to drive the enemy out of the streets of Velletri and climb within sight of Rome. Behind him lie the dead towns that will never rise again. Yet the first thing he glimpses is only a dome. In the modern measure it is neither immense nor very high; as he nears the town it will sink into the mass of low buildings following the contours of the hills. Seen close, it is dwarfed by the facade of St. Peter's Church. But by some magic Michelangelo fashioned something that seems to float in the air, and after four centuries so dominates the approaches that it remains the first thing to be seen from any direction.

In the Alban hills the armies are really in the suburbs of Rome.

Yet between the hills and the city gates a great drama will be played out. A momentous decision will be taken. Will the Germans defend the capital? Will the battle be carried into the streets of Rome—into the Forum, up the steps of the Capitoline, where the bronze Marcus Aurelius waits, into the crude little churches of the Via Appia that follow the footsteps of St. Paul and his first disciples, into the colonnade of St. Peter's? Will Augustus' Altar of Peace be once more broken into bits and another Nero watch the burning of Rome from his Magic Mountain, so much higher than the Pincio?

This is the question that hangs over the Campagna as the weary G.I.'s catch their first glimpse of Rome. The city they are fighting for is not a great fortress. It has no military value except as a communications center. When they reach it they will be far from the end of the bloody trail they are blazing to victory. It is a famished city, the Pope says in his anguished appeal to the belligerents to spare it.

Nevertheless it will be a great conquest. Rome is a Golden Milestone as truly as it was in the days when all the roads of the western world met at the foot of the Capitol. In the intensity of world interest focused upon this spot, in the special significance attached to its capture by the fighting men, it is clear that this battle is thought of as one of the decisive engagements of the war. People who care less than nothing for Rome as the cradle of Christendom or the headquarters of the Catholic Church, people indifferent to it as the living record of our civilization, people allergic to historic monuments and artistic treasures, strategists who consider Italy a secondary or diversionary front, and wait with tense nerves for the grand assault elsewhere—even these cannot help sensing that the fate of the Eternal City has an importance all its own.

The nearer it approaches the more evident it is that the battle for Rome has to be a symbolic battle. Its peculiar character is underlined by the voice of the Pope, rising out of the beleaguered and otherwise silent city on the eve of the final contest. During most of his address to the Cardinals, the Pontiff spoke as Bishop of Rome and head of the Church. His impassioned hope that Rome will be spared will be echoed in all the Allied countries. Mr. Churchill hinted in his latest speech that there was a chance that it would not be fought over. This might mean that some understanding has been reached, or that the Germans are known to be withdrawing, in which case there will certainly be no attack on our side.

In the concluding portion of his discourse the Pope did not advocate a compromise peace or declare, as quoted in some of the headlines, that a demand for total victory would prolong the war. He begged for a just and merciful peace after victory, after "a just atonement for violent acts." His words on this subject sound like a condemnation of Dr. Goebbels' propaganda, which aims to make people believe that the victors desire the "total destruction" of the vanquished. It is "those who feel and fear lest nations and peoples as such would have no other alternative besides this—full victory or complete destruction * * * " who give cause for the prolongation of the war. They "advance as in a hynotic sleep * * * and compel all the remainder to a bloody and exhausting struggle." "It is therefore of capital importance that fear should be superseded by a reasonable expectation of honest solutions." The Pope says little more than Mr. Churchill and Mr. Roosevelt said to Italy and that both Allied leaders have repeated in their statements respecting the future order of the world.

16

POSITION OF POPE IN ITALY
HAS BEEN ENHANCED BY WAR

August 21, 1944

One of the most interesting changes that have taken place in Italy during the war is that in the position of the Pope.

With the revival of political parties and the restoration of freedom of expression a certain amount of dormant anti-clericalism has come to the surface. Masonry, long a political factor in this country has risen from the underground with other anti-Fascist forces. But Fascist extremists like Roberto Farinacci had specialized for so many years in attacks on the church that they had stolen some of the thunder of the traditional anti-clericals, just as Benito Mussolini's strident "Fascist Republicans" in the north incline ardent republicans in the liberated territory to hold the monarchic question in suspense for the transition period.

So far, however, Italy's painful struggle to come to life again has not been marked by the violent polemics that embittered politics between 1870 and the First World War.

The parties are enjoying this luxury, but the tone of the argument is surprisingly sober and restrained. The coalition Government is playing the minor, subservient role assigned to it by the Allied Control Commission and is sincerely seeking unity and reconciliation. In particular, there is no disposition to reopen the "Roman Question" or rescind the Lateran Treaty.

Count Carlo Sforza reflected the disposition of his colleagues in the Government, Left as well as Right, when he said in his speech today: "In 1915 an Italian statesmen imposed in agreements for future peace a formula needlessly offensive to the highest spiritual authority existing in Italy and the world. Today such a policy would offend the spirit of any Italian, because today all Italians share the feeling of heartfelt gratitude for the action of a church that, as in 'Carroccio' times, has so often and nobly helped patriots fighting for the cause of Italy, which is also the cause of Christian civilization."

This attitude is largely due to the extraordinary popularity of the present Pontiff. Presiding over a world-wide church in a world-wide war that is also a civil and religious war, Pius XII comes out of the ordeal a stronger figure, as far as liberated Italy is concerned, than he was before. An old liberal, commenting today on the place of the Christian Democratic party in the coalition, said: "The last thing that I expected in the crisis was the resurgence of the Catholic party in greater force than the Communists and Socialists. An equally surprising phenomenon is the rising prestige of the Pope.

Mussolini has gone, the King has gone, and nobody mourns. The Pope remains the winner of Italy's one victory—the saving of Rome."

The Romans give credit to the Pontiff for the sparing of the city. It gives them added reason to desire to perpetuate the neutral status of the Vatican. But this is not the only cause for the popularity of Pius XII. During the nine months between the armistice and the entry into Rome, the Vatican was a refuge for thousands of fugitives from the Nazi-Fascist reign of terror. Jews received first priority—Italian Jews and Jews who escaped here from Germany and other occupied countries—but all the hunted found sanctuary in the Vatican and its hundreds of convents and monasteries in the Rome region.

What the Pope did was to create an attitude in favor of the persecuted and hunted that the city was quick to adopt, so that hiding someone "on the run" became the thing to do. This secret sharing of danger cleared away fascism more effectively than an official purge. The Vatican is still sheltering refugees. Almost 100,000 homeless persons from the war zone and devastated areas are fed there every day.

It has also had an effect on the Pontiff himself. Compared to four years ago, when he looked oppressed and agonized by the tragedy that he had been powerless to avert, today Pope Pius seems strengthened and revitalized. He attributes this in part to the great comfort and refreshment of spirit that he derives from the throngs of Allied soldiers who crowd the audience chambers of the Vatican every day. Yesterday he received 3,000, mostly boys from the United States, who trooped up the Scala Regia nudging one another and trying to look nonchalant.

Almost every day, too, the Pope gives a private audience to some American visitor—a general, a Cabinet officer, an envoy on a special mission, an occasional journalist. Since Rome's liberation he has probably talked with more Americans than during his whole pontificate.

These talks in the crimson-and-gold papal study are often long and remarkably frank. The Pope gives no interviews, but he answers questions freely and asks a great many pertinent questions himself. By now he must be pretty familiar with the American point of view on most problems of war and peace. From the beginning of the war he has been preoccupied with the shape of the peace. As victory approaches, this interest is naturally intensified.

The idea that the Pope does not want a complete and decisive victory is erroneous. What concerns him is the policy to be pursued by the victors after the decision has been won. As a spiritual ruler he can hardly be expected to take the same view as the military and political leaders.

17

POPE'S BROADCAST
INTERESTS ALLIED CIRCLES

September 6, 1944

Great interest is taken in Allied circles here in the Pope's broadcast on the fifth anniversary of the war. Particular attention has been given to the concluding passages referring to world organization. The Pontiff has exchanged views with so many Allied leaders since Rome's liberation that it would not be surprising if his thought was colored by their ideas of the future. It is not fortuitous at any rate that while the Dumbarton Oaks* conference was engaged in laying foundations for a new international security system Pius XII seized the opportunity to support efforts of "the architects" who are

* Dumbarton Oaks conference held in Washington, D.C. between U.S., U.S.S.R. and United Kingdom. Proposed organization of nations for maintenance of world peace. This led to the calling of the United Nations Conference in 1945, where the charter was signed June 26 by fifty nations.

drawing essential plans for the new world which must rise on the ruins of the old.

"Already in our Christmas message of 1939," said His Holiness, "we expressed the desire for creation of an international organization which while avoiding the lacunae and defects of the past should be really capable of preserving peace according to principles of justice and equity against all possible threats in the future. Since today in the light of terrible experience the desire to secure a new world-wide peace institution of this kind is ever more occupying the attention and care of statesman and peoples we gladly express our pleasure and firm hope that its actual achievement may really correspond in the largest possible measure to the nobility of its end, which is maintenance of tranquility and security in the world for the benefit of all."

This is interpreted as evidence that the Pontiff has accepted the postulates of Allied victory. Certainly his words carry no suggestion of a plea for a negotiated peace. Some observers read into the Pope's statement a bid for a place for the Vatican in an international organization, but this idea received no support from a high church official interrogated on this point last week by this correspondent. "It is very unlikely," he said, "that the church would consent to take part in a body inevitably involved in political questions of the most controversial character. Besides, such an organization to be effective must be backed by force, and the Holy See could not and would not invoke any but moral power."

The Holy Father's words may be regarded rather as endorsement of the "American peace plan," for the scheme of organization discussed at Dumbarton Oaks is regarded here as a United States formula.

If so, Vatican support is a diplomatic triumph for Myron

Taylor, the President's personal representative to the Holy
See. Mr. Taylor sees the Pope more often than any other foreign diplomat and since, as adviser to the State Department,
he helped formulate the plan for world organization, it is
easy to guess that the chief object of his mission to the Vatican at this decisive hour is to enlist the Pope's moral backing
and influence in the Catholic world for American peace aims.

At the war's beginning the Pontiff declared himself in
favor of an international body to maintain peace. In his latest
utterance he asserts that this body should be "really capable
of preserving the peace against all possible threat," which
means he accepts the thesis that "adequate force" must be
maintained to secure peace.

Italians were struck by the unusual tone and language of
the broadcast. They commented on the departure from ecclesiastical style, especially in passages referring to conditions in
Italy. When before, they ask, has a Pope spoken of such concrete and current matters as requisitioning, black markets,
transport difficulties?

The Pope sounded the alarm all responsible voices are
raising here regarding the threatening consequences of "misery, famine, unemployment and economic unrest." He is
understood to have spoken in the same sense to Churchill and
to have found the Prime Minister well informed and anxious
about conditions in Italy.

From the testimony of those who talked to both after their
meeting, it appears that the Pontiff and the British leader, so
different in background, experience and outlook, greatly impressed one another. The Pope is said to have described
Churchill as "very able and large-minded," while Churchill
admired the Pope's "simplicity, sincerity and power." No
doubt the Pontiff's knowledge of the desperate plight of the

Italian people impressed the Prime Minister and rounded out reports that he had heard on all sides. One reason for his change of attitude toward Italy is the decided trend toward communism he must have observed even in the most conservative part of the country. Russia is Italy's alternative to Anglo-American friendship, as the Russians are suggesting in all kinds of unobtrusive ways. Reconciled as he is to Soviet influence on one side of the Adriatic, Mr. Churchill does not relish it on both sides.

The Pope is even more aware of this tendency, not only in Italy but throughout Europe. Without mentioning communism in his broadcast, he made a persuasive defense of private property—one institution the land-hungry peasants of this continent instinctively support—at the same time condemning a capitalism which assumes "unlimited right over property" and that "excessive concentration of economic goods often hidden under anonymous titles" which saves them from contributing to the social order and makes it impossible for the worker to acquire private property of his own.

Most impressive of all, however, coming from the age-old pulpit of St. Peter's, was the Pope's recognition that the war is nearly over, that the old world lies in fragments, and that the wise or unwise rulers of today are charged with the responsibility to draw plans for a new world.

18

PAPAL MESSAGE A MOMENTOUS PRONOUNCEMENT

December 25, 1944

The Pope's Christmas message is an extraordinary document considered simply as a papal pronouncement. In the time, circumstances and setting in which it is delivered it stands out as one of the historic utterances of the war. For when the head of the Catholic Church tells the world that the peoples of the earth call for a system of government in "keeping with the dignity and liberty of the citizens," when he testifies that the world would not have been dragged into war if there had not existed a "concentration of dictatorial power," when he concludes, "We must vest efficient guarantees in the people itself" to avoid repetition of such a catastrophe, he declares democracy the best and safest form of government. This is a testament and judgment of the highest importance. It cuts through the moral confusion that has developed as the conflict spread and brings it back to the immense and simple, the elemental issue for which millions of men are fighting.

The Pope speaks on the sixth Christmas of the war. While from his high vantage point at the dead center of the storm he suggests the end will come "sooner than people think," observers on a lower plane see no immediate prospect of a German collapse or surrender. It is true that the position of a large part of Europe is incomparably better this Christmas than last. "At least we can breathe this year," the rector of Rome University told the writer a few days ago. "We are by way of becoming free men again. That is a great victory we have won out of defeat." Nevertheless, the sixth Christmas is a thin, hungry, cold Christmas for most of the liberated, a homesick, sad Christmas for liberating armies, a bitter Christmas heavy with hope too long deferred for those waiting to be delivered.

Pius XII speaks in this atmosphere. He speaks from the capital of a ruined country still cut in half by the battleline, and he cannot help being affected by the misery and the simmering revolt of Italy. Yet when he refers to people awakening from a "long torpor" he can also find an example in the first stirrings of energy and hope in this country. This correspondent has just returned from a brief visit to Florence to observe what has happened to the city and the countryside in three months of liberation. Arno is a more painful sight than before, because clearing away the debris reveals the extent of irreparable damage. The population is colder and hungrier because there is no fuel and almost nothing to supplement the bread ration of 200 grams daily. But there are light and water, and craftsmen are resuming work with scraps of material available. Above all, there is more spirit.

This is the background of the Pope's message. More important, it reflects all he has seen from his unique observation post in the middle of the battlefield during more than five years of war. He has seen three occupations of Rome: Fascist, Nazi and Allied. Having observed the effect of dictatorship at closest range, now he has seen the work and fruits of democracy at first hand. In the last six months especially he has been in daily contact with representatives of democracy— statesmen, officers, thousands upon thousands of Allied troopers.

Perhaps it is too much to say the Pontiff's verdict comes out of this experience and observation. Nevertheless, it is a verdict perhaps more momentous in a moral sense than any decision of the war. On this Christmas Eve, after an Advent devoted to prayer and meditation, the head of a world-wide church takes sides for democracy against dictatorship or any existing form of absolute government, not on political but on moral, spiritual and human grounds. This is a deeply pondered pontifical pronouncement in favor of democracy in the interests of the "individual himself, who so far from being the object and a merely passive element in the social order is in fact and must be and continue to be its subject, its foundation and its end."

The Pontiff's definition of the rights and duties of citizens and their representatives in a democracy, and especially the distinction he makes between the people and the masses— between a shapeless multitude moved from outside and conscious citizens living by their own energy, conscious of their own life-energy and own views—are worth careful study.

So are the ideas of Pius XII on an effective peace organization. For the Pope not only supports a democratic solution of national problems; he comes out strongly in favor of an international body with power to use force if necessary to preserve peace. Democracy, he says wisely, demands "moral maturing" of the citizen, and international society is based on the moral necessity of recognizing the unity of mankind. On the thorny question of national sovereignty he makes a real contribution when he declares that the authority of such a society must be real and effective over member states in such a manner that "each of them retains an equal right to its own sovereignty."

Obviously, if all give up the same prerogatives so that one nation is not more powerful than others in joint decisions, the chief obstacle to real cooperation would be surmounted. The Pontiff's views on world organization are definite and comprehensive. He favors international as well as national democracy. In every respect, in short, this is a remarkable declaration from the Vatican. It will have an enormous effect on the minds not only of Catholics on both sides of the battle-line but on all men of good-will everywhere.

19

INFLUENCE OF VATICAN POLICY
SHOWS IN ITALY

December 26, 1945

The extent to which the Vatican policy overshadows the policy of Italy at the present juncture is evident in the great stir created in diplomatic circles in Rome by the revolutionary transformation announced on Christmas Eve in the character and composition of the College of Cardinals. Under Allied control the Italian Government has still so little real power that the recent crisis bored everybody but the politicians involved. But when the Supreme Council of the Catholic Church is extended so that for the first time the preponderance passes away from Italy while the traditional confines of Christendom are enlarged to take in representatives from China, Africa and the "new lands" of the Western Hemi-

sphere, the departure arouses the keenest interest among observers of the international trend.

Pope Pius XII is a cautious but persistent innovator. He
is as much secretary of state today as when he held the office
under his predecessor and he will continue to direct the Vatican foreign policy after he fills that now vacant post. The
world is his parish and thanks to the fortunes of war he has
exchanged views with more laymen of different creeds and
nationalities than any pontiff of modern times. Because of
these outside contacts as well as the reports flowing in daily
from every diocese he has a wider perspective than most secular rulers on the changes the war has wrought and is more
alive to the necessity of adapting old institutions to new conditions.

This is the meaning of the break with precedent in the
new nominations to the Electoral College. It is a consequence
of the war. The head of the Church is chosen by the Cardinals from among themselves, so that each new member is a
potential Pope and is designated with that in mind. For centuries all Popes have been Italians. By reducing the proportion of Italian Cardinals—now twenty-eight to forty-two—the
present pontiff has not only made it possible but easier to
elect a non-Italian.

He has suggested that tradition is not unbreakable and that
in existing circumstances a change might better serve what he
referred to again and again in his Christmas allocution as
the "supranational" nature and mission of the Church. Foreign diplomats regard this move as highly significant. "Pius
XII," says a representative of a country which has no envoy
to the Holy See, "has written a new page in the long story of
the adaptability of the Catholic Church."

Some European critics see in the new list of Cardinals a

tendency toward the "Americanization" of the Church. They point out that the largest group of nominees from any one country comes from the United States, that Canada with a comparatively small Catholic population will now have two Cardinals and that Cuba, Chile and Peru will vote for the first time in a papal election.

The appointment of Bishop Joseph P. Hurley of St. Augustine as papal envoy to Yugoslavia is regarded as a further sign of this trend. Certainly this is an important and delicate mission for an American prelate. Bishop Hurley is an experienced diplomat, the first American official member of the Vatican Secretariat of State. He goes as the representative of the Holy See to the westernmost outpost of the Soviet "sphere." His acceptance by Marshal Tito implies to most observers here that he has the tacit approval of Moscow. Since it is obvious that an Italian legate would not be *persona grata* in Belgrade it will be interesting to see what an American can do in a post where new problems of political adjustment are no thornier than old differences between the eastern and western churches.

But with fourteen Cardinals from the Americas as against fifty-one in Europe the process of Americanization has a long way to go. And Bishop Hurley's mission is more significant as a consequence of the war than as a sign that Americans are playing a bigger part in Vatican diplomacy. Proof that the war has influenced the Pope's choices is written large not only in the fact that new countries have a voice in the Sacred College but also in the persons selected for the church's highest honor.

The three new German Cardinals were all outspoken critics of the Nazi regime. The outstanding nominee in France is the venerable Archbishop Saliege of Toulouse, noted for his defiance of the Germans and the collaborationists.* Archbishop Sapieha of Cracow is a courageous patriot who shared all the suffering of his people. Archbishop Mindszenty of Hungary was a prisoner of the Nazis.

There is another point. During the Fascist regime Mussolini tried to revive the greatness of the Roman Empire. For a gaudy interval he succeeded in keeping the spotlight on himself and making Italy a key factor in world politics. For fifty years before that, while Italian unity was being forged at the expense of the temporal power of the Popes, Rome was chiefly interesting as a center of a national movement. Now the Mussolini melodrama is an almost forgotten thriller that had its macabre finale in a Milan gas station. Because of defeat and its virtual loss of independence Italy as a nation swings no weight in the international scale.

Today the only international center in Rome is the Vatican. Almost as in the days of the papal states but more so. The Pope is the pontifex maximus, the great figure in the Eternal City. And Pius XII, gathering around him representatives from the four quarters of the earth, is working to make Rome once more an international capital.

* Archbishop Saliege was decorated by the American Jewish Committee for saving the lives of so many Jews during the Nazi occupation of France; Archbishop Sapieha died as a formidable opponent of the Nazis; Archbishop Mindszenty recently received asylum in the American Embassy in Hungary.

20

THE CENTRAL FIGURE IN THE
ROMAN PAGEANT

February 20, 1946

Among the prelates who will receive the Red Hat today in the long Hall of the Benedictions, above the porch of St. Peter's, none will derive as much satisfaction from the great occasion as the Bishop and son of Rome who has summoned them from the five continents to take part in a new and spectacular affirmation of the universal character and mission of the Catholic Church. Pope Pius XII is the central figure of a pageant as old as the world's oldest senate. He is presiding over a traditional ceremonial that actually ushers in an utmost revolutionary change—revolutionary because by broadening the base of elections to the Papacy it is bound to influence the governing mind of the church.

No one is more aware of these implications than the Pope

himself. In an audience granted to this correspondent last New Year's Eve he spoke with great emphasis of the "necessity" of transforming the College of Cardinals into a more truly international body. He said he had been pondering over it all through the war. But he never mentioned the word "international," nor has that term appeared in the announcement of the nominations on Christmas Eve or the brief allocution at the secret Consistory on Monday.

The words used are "universal" and "supranational." It is as if Pius XII wishes to distinguish between the spiritual idea of universality and the current political connotations of nationalism and internationalism. Even the latter term as applied at present to UNO has a limited and exclusive application compared to his definition of the universal church: "This church does not belong to one race or to one people or nation, but to all peoples of the human family."

The deep satisfaction felt by Pius XII in effecting the change was evident in his words and manner. It takes courage to break with tradition in the atmosphere of the Vatican, where the measure of time and of judgment is not so much slower as larger than it is in secular seats of government. The Pope's study is a very quiet room at the end of a long series of crimson and gold reception rooms, each a little smaller than the last, each a little emptier of people waiting, so that by the time you reach the book-lined chamber where the Pontiff in his white cassock sits alone at his desk, the outer world has receded somewhat. It is the same world because the Pope at his crowded desk is terribly close to it, but the perspective is different.

On New Year's Eve an American general was received in farewell audience just before his return to the United States.

He hurried toward the audience chamber at a kind of military quickstep, but he came out lingeringly and walked slowly down the long line of doors guarded by papal chamberlains. In the Pope's presence you understand that easing up of speed and tension. He receives many visitors in the course of a morning, each with a different interest, a different background, but he is never hurried. Sitting or standing, he is straight, strong, taut as a watch spring, thin as a young tree, but tranquil and tranquilizing—a Gothic figure whose vestments fall around him in Gothic folds, whose long hands are raised in Gothic gestures, both stiff and graceful.

The kind of questions he asks of his constant procession of visitors is as remarkable as the kind of confidences he inspires. When the old Cardinals, mostly Italians, gave their "placet" * to his decision to de-Italianize the electoral college, it was in resigned acknowledgment of the change that the defeat of Italy and the decline of Europe have wrought in the world and in the outlook of the Catholic Church. The Pope had talked it over with most of them during the war years. So, while it caused a stir in ecclesiastical as well as political circles in Rome, the churchmen were prepared to accept the view that it is necessary.

The Italians, or at least the Romans, perceive some compensation for what they somberly refer to as the "complete eclipse" of Italy in the thought that a light still shines in Rome. An old anti-clerical, a leader of the Action party, made this wry comment when the Consistory was announced: "The Popes fought for years to keep Rome from being the national capital in order to preserve it as the capital of the church. Today I think the only statesman left us is the Pope.

* "Approval."

I suppose Italians ought to be grateful that Rome is the capital of something."

New Yorkers take an interest in the ceremonial in Rome because the Archbishop of New York is raised to the Cardinalate. But New York has had a Cardinal before in the person of Cardinal Hayes. Chicago has had Cardinal Mundelein. But now there are Cardinals in Detroit and St. Louis, which means that the importance of the Middle West is recognized in that quiet watch tower where Pius XII looks over the world. It means that the representatives of the Catholics of the Mississippi Valley will now cast three votes in Papal elections. This brings home the significance of the change in the College of Cardinals.

21

THE LETTERS
OF PRESIDENT ROOSEVELT
TO POPE PIUS XII

April 12, 1947

Published on the second anniversary of his death, the letters*
written by Franklin D. Roosevelt to Pope Pius XII throw an
interesting light on the mind and character of the late President as well as on the purpose that inspired his rather bold
initiative in appointing a personal representative to the Holy
See. The correspondence began shortly after the war started,
and the first letter, dated Dec. 23, 1939, reveals that Roosevelt foresaw that every force in the world, and particularly
the moral and spiritual forces, would have to be mobilized
before the struggle was over.

The battle at that time was hardly joined and two years

---

* *Franklin D. Roosevelt and Pius XII*, Wartime correspondence; introduction by Myron C. Taylor. Macmillan, April, 1947.

were to pass before the United States became an open combatant, but even then he was thinking of the peace and of his own part in the peace. He did not want to miss any opportunity or ignore any factor that could be used in weaving the Grand Design that was already taking shape in his imagination. It was the post-war period, the time he did not live to see, that dominated his thoughts. It was in anticipation of that time that he decided to seek, he wrote, "a closer association between those in every part of the world—those in religion and those in government—who have a common purpose."

The letters to the Pope are unique in disclosing the religious turn of Roosevelt's mind, which became more apparent in his profound anxieties as the war neared an end. They show him also in the more familiar attitude of looking far ahead and far afield. In the darkest hours he never doubted the outcome of the war or that his ideas would prevail in the peace. The motive of this correspondence was to enlist the support of the head of the Catholic Church for these basic ideas.

Throughout the war the Pope thought only of peace. His letters are no less revealing than the President's. They show his anguish of spirit and the emotion as "for providential help" with which he welcomed the opportunity for an intimate exchange of views with the President.

When Russia entered the war and before we were in, Roosevelt made one of his most persuasive efforts to convince the Supreme Pontiff that the Soviet dictatorship was less dangerous that the Nazi regime. He argued that "the survival of Russia is less dangerous to religion, to the church as such, and to humanity in general than would be the survival of the German form of dictatorship." The result was an allocution reiterating the Church's stand on atheistic communism and freedom of worship, but laying particular emphasis on the Pope's sympathy and regard for the Russian people.

It goes without saying that the Pope and the President did not see eye to eye on many subjects. The differences in their position and outlook were profound. But they had much in common, especially in their ideas of peace, and the principles which the President expressed in his messages and the Pontiff enthusiastically accepted as his own represented Roosevelt's real aims and hopes. They were battered down by the war pressures, but in this correspondence they appear shining and whole.

The two leaders met in Hyde Park when Cardinal Pacelli was Secretary of State and in the correspondence the acquaintance developed into friendship and respect. The President addressed the Pope as "my old and good friend," and the Pope always refers to the President with lively affection. Much that passed between them is not recorded. Mr. Taylor, whose introduction and explanatory notes provide the background of time and circumstance in which the messages were written, speaks of his good fortune in having been chosen to be "the means of conveying from one to the other the innermost thoughts of two men of such eminence." As intermediary he played an important role and his reports of the conversations he transmitted are needed to complete the story of a relationship of great human and historic significance.

Officially, it was strictly a person-to-person relationship. Mr. Taylor's mission was not to the Vatican, a microscopic but independent state to which nearly all existing governments send Ambassadors, but to the Pontiff himself. Mr.

Roosevelt was in the habit of using personal envoys for special purposes. Mr. Taylor was serving in this capacity on the Intergovernmental Committee on Political Refugees when he was asked to undertake the mission to Rome. The appointment caused no stir at the time, probably because the first letter to the Pope coincided with messages asking leaders of the Protestant and Jewish faiths to cooperate in meeting the shock of war and building a foundation for peace.

Since hostilities ended, however, representatives of some Protestant denominations have protested against Mr. Taylor's mission on the ground that in some unexplained way it cuts across the policy of separation of church and state. This record may be published to answer the critics. Certainly it furnishes no support to their contention. President Truman contributes a preface stating that it is given to the world "in the American tradition of open diplomacy."

Published today, the correspondence underlines how far we are from the fulfillment of the aims the late President shared with Pius XII. It justifies Roosevelt's foresight in face of a moral and spiritual crisis and conflict greater than he or anyone else could have foreseen while the war lasted. What is needed now is more cooperation among religious bodies, more unity among the churches.

22

THE PERSPECTIVE OF A MAN
OF ANOTHER WORLD

February 12, 1949

This morning the small police force of the microscopic state of Vatican City, very decorative in sweeping black capes lined with purple, stood at attention on the road leading to St. Peter's. A few thousand people gathered in the square and a scattering of flags, mostly on government buildings, flew over the Roman streets. The occasion for this mild display was the official visit of Premier de Gasperi to the Pope on the occasion of the twentieth anniversary of the signing of the Lateran Treaty.

This was de Gasperi's first visit to Pius XII as Prime Minister. Once before, when the Republic was proclaimed, he accompanied Provisional President de Nicola to the Vatican on a formal call of notification. Otherwise His Holiness and

the former Vatican librarian have not met since de Gasperi
entered the Government. Both are extremely anxious not to
give ground to charges of Vatican influence on the Christian
Democratic party which de Gasperi heads.

His Holiness and the Prime Minister conversed together
for fifty minutes this morning. No doubt they wasted little
time on the Lateran Pact, for the remarkable thing about this
agreement is that nobody thinks about it any more. The famous "Roman Question," for sixty years the burning issue in
Italian politics, is practically forgotten. The Lateran Treaty
is the work of Mussolini, and many contend it could not have
been put over except by a dictator. Perhaps not, but it has
survived Fascism and the fall of the Monarchy. It was incorporated in the Constitution of the Republic with the unani-
mous support of all parties, including the Communists.
Twenty years after, not a voice in Italy is raised against it.

The Pontiff naturally referred to the Lateran Treaty in the
audience accorded to this correspondent following the reception to the Prime Minister and his entourage. To the Holy
See the advantage of the act of reconciliation with the Italian
Government is not simply in giving the Pope sovereignty
over the Vatican grounds and St. Peter's Cathedral. Nor is
it in regulating the long-confused relations between Church
and State in Italy and defining the limits of civil and ecclesiastical authority. Its main benefit is in guaranteeing the
Vatican independence to function as an international institution.

This is the present Pontiff's chief concern. The relation of
the Church in Italy and the National Government is one
thing, to be determined by mutual agreement of purely local
scope. Concordats are in force in many countries. Freedom to

act as the head of a universal church is another and far more important thing in the eyes of the Pope. The great value of a territorial toehold in a friendly country is that it insures the right of free communication between the Supreme Pontiff and his world-wide flock.

This right is the more highly valued the more it is abrogated. The Vatican is sunk in gloom these days by the tragedy of Cardinal Mindszenty and the gloom and tragedy are deepened because the doomed Primate is completely cut off from communication with the Holy See. This is the first time the Soviet power has struck at the College of Cardinals, the governing body of the Church and the Pope's official family, and the blow is regarded here as a terrorizing threat to the entire hierarchy of the satellite states. Already every Bishop of the Uniate Church in Rumania (affiliated with Rome) is in jail. News of arrests of priests arrives daily at the Vatican.

The Pope shows marks of the strain he is suffering. His pale, mobile face is more deeply lined than it was last year, but the lines are of sorrow more than of age. Ten years a Pope on March 2, the burden of the papacy in as critical a decade as it has ever experienced weighs visibly on his frail shoulders. But he stands erect under the load. He walks, talks and gestures with the vivacity of a man half his age. He has steel-spring resilience and his dark eyes flash with interest in everything.

In words that cannot, unfortunately, be quoted, he talked this morning on such a variety of subjects as Western defense, the fate of China (a matter of profound anxiety in the Vatican), land reform in Italy, the plight of the world's suffering and abandoned children, the war in Greece, the progress of ERP and the future of Germany. He manifested an especially keen interest in conditions in the Near East and the prospects in Israel. From conversations here and in Tel Aviv it is fair to guess that recognition and the exchange of representatives between the two States is not far off.

Pius XII is not tired by the innumerable audiences he gives, because he likes people. He is fifty years a priest this year and as he looks back on his long career it is obvious that although most of it has been spent as Diplomat, Secretary of State and Supreme Pontiff, in his own mind he is always a Parish Priest with an ever widening Parish. The Church he heads is undergoing a terrible ordeal and he suffers all the agonies of all his flock—suffers and at the same time accepts them, for he expects the faithful to be martyrs. He is described as a man of the world because he is more accessible than most Popes and shows a lively interest in periods and events. But actually he is a man of another world with a quite different perspective from other statesmen of his time because he looks so far beyond it.

23

ROME AT THE HALFWAY POINT
OF THE HOLY YEAR

July 10, 1950

The great piazza in front of Saint Peter's has become a parking place for autobuses. Lined up within the encircling arms of the ancient colonnade are hundreds of shiny red and blue vehicles, all apparently brand-new, that bring thousands of pilgrims each day to the steps of the Basilica. All Rome is in the streets in the long twilights of these burning days. The old city never looked so crowded and lively. But nowhere are people and movement concentrated all day long as in the broad avenue that replaces the narrow lanes with a new ceremonial approach from the Tiber to the vast church and the dwarfed palaces that constitute the strange little state called Vatican City. Lighted by rows of pylons and flanked by new buildings, the avenue is criticized by the captious as too modern for the setting until they hear it was planned that way by Michelangelo when he built the dome.

In those days the faithful who traveled to the Eternal City for the Jubilee* came mostly on foot. Even today a few pilgrims, not only from Italian villages but from as far away as England, walk the same roads that always led to Rome. But they are a small minority. More come by air and rail—special trains shuttle back and forth daily from Frankfurt, for instance—and a small number by private car. The big majority, however, arrive by bus. Yesterday one saw busloads from places as far apart as Cairo, Vienna, Nice, London, Calcutta, Algiers and Georgetown University. Today a young nun from Ecuador was raised to sainthood in the last canonization ceremony of the Jubilee year, and while the people most in evidence were from Spain, Cuba and South America, there were buses filled with handsome black pilgrims from Central Africa and others bright with the saris of ladies from India.

The feature of the trek to Rome for the Holy Year indeed is that it is a pilgrimage by bus. The pilgrims are conveyed from church to church by bus and when their devotions are over these handy conveyances take them to see the animals in the zoo or hear the music in the Baths of Caracalla.

They are not too pious to enjoy the greatest experience some of them have ever had. Yesterday while the immense nave of Saint Peter's resounded with hymns sung in a multitude of tongues and prayers from thousands of voices beat upon the dome in a wave of supplication—"O Lord, give us peace, make us worthy of peace"—a beaming little woman

---

* A year of special prayer which begins and ends with the opening and closing of the holy door in St. Peter's on consecutive Christmas eves, has historical precedent in the year of jubilee prescribed for the Jews by God (Lev. 25:10-15). The Holy Year has been proclaimed every twenty-five years since 1450.

from a Calabrian village whispered to an American on the fringes of the throng that she had a brother in Bridgeport, Conn. "You are an American, and over there I met a boy from Tunis," she said happily. "What a wonderful place to see the world."

To all these pilgrims this is the Mother Church and wherever they come from they feel at home in it. Their common faith and purpose make them feel at home with one another. The lights, the music, the religious pageantry, the white figure of the Pope as he holds his mass audiences in the square, move them deeply but awe them no more than the giant statues in Saint Peter's awe the small boys who sit astride their feet. In a very palpable sense, to repeat, they feel they have traveled far to come home.

Halfway through the Holy Year the Romans complain that the crowds are less than they expected, and though no trips have yet been canceled they fear that alarm over Korea will frighten off many who planned to come later. Certainly the visitors to the shrine of the Apostles do not add much to the revenue of the best hotels or the Roman shops. More than twenty-two thousand of the forty thousand the city can accommodate are housed in hostels organized by the Vatican. One exception is the Palazzo Salviati, a fine Renaissance building formerly used as a school for army officers, which was turned into a hostel by the Government with the aid of E. C. A. funds and will eventually become a youth center. Another is an auto camp for motoring pilgrims provided by the Rome Automobile Club. In addition there are a few tent colonies for boys, and several unused factories in the suburbs were transformed into dormitories for the record throngs that came here at Easter and Whitsuntide.

But most pilgrims are sheltered in religious houses or colleges like the Leoneana, which has distributed its students in other places to make room for eight hundred fifty Holy Year guests. In these houses the rates are very low, and all, including the monasteries, have been equipped for the duration with bars, barber shops and souvenir shops where the visitors can spend the little they have to spend.

Even the Communists, who hate the sight of these praying pilgrims, admit that the Holy Year has not failed to attract devotees from the ends of the earth. Although much of the Catholic world is cut off from communication if not from communion with Rome, more than a million have found their way here so far—the largest number from France, the second largest number from Germany. Their presence neither overwhelms nor enriches Rome, it creates an atmosphere very different from that of other capitals. Here the centers of activity are not the Chamber of Deputies, the usual haunts of the tourists, or the sidewalk cafes that jam the Via Veneto, they are the churches: Saint Peter's and the major basilicas where the pilgrims congregate. It is a new experience for a political reporter to come to a capital and find that its outstanding feature is not politics but prayer.

24

VATICAN'S ATTITUDE
TOWARD AMERICAN RELATIONS

December 24, 1951

The proposal to appoint an American Ambassador to the Holy See causes much less excitement at the Vatican than in the United States. Announcement that President Truman will proceed with his intention of submitting the name of General Mark Clark for the new post when the Senate reconvenes next month evoked no comment in Vatican City. Outside the narrow limits of the Papal domain, astir with preparations for the joyous pageantry of Christmas, some Romans question the choice of an active general as envoy to the Holy See. But church officials have nothing to say on this or any other aspect of the matter. The Vatican was not advised in advance or consulted on the appointment, and its attitude is that it is strictly the business of the United States.

It is clear, however, that under this discreet silence there is surprise at the amount and violence of American opposition to the President's move. Church officials say emphatically that it would be better not to have an Ambassador than to stir up sectarian feeling and religious controversy in the United States. It is understood that this is the view of the Pope himself.

From the church's standpoint it is logical. The position of the Catholic Church in the United States and the relations of Catholic Americans with their fellow citizens of other faiths are more important to the Holy See than the presence here of a representative of the American Government. The establishment of official diplomatic relations would certainly be welcome—but as a favor to the church. In Vatican circles the idea prevails that the chief advantages of the mission would fall on the American side.

They feel that the appointment of Myron Taylor as the President's personal representative to the Pope was motivated by Roosevelt's interest in maintaining a listening post in Rome in wartime. The mission proved valuable in keeping the Holy See in touch with American policy and public opinion and in opening to Washington sources of information not otherwise available at that time.

When the war was over thousands of American officers, soldiers, officials and visitors of all faiths were received by the Pope, largely because it was easy for an American representative accredited to the Vatican to arrange the audiences. This was the period of "open house" at the Vatican, when Pius XII met more Americans than any other Pontiff in history or any living ruler.

Audiences are not so easy now. Catholics usually apply

through the American College, but other visitors miss the good offices of Mr. Taylor and his State Department aide, Franklin Gowen. This is particularly true of officials who desire to see the Holy Father for one reason or another. Our Embassy to the Italian Government is not a channel of communication with the Vatican and in several instances American officials have either refrained from asking for an audience or their indirect request has been courteously turned down because there is no diplomatic officer to present them.

In any event the day of the "personal representative" is past. The abrupt manner in which the Taylor mission was ended, without previous notification to the Vatican, shocked a Pontiff who is himself a diplomat, and of the old school that sets great store on good manners. Since then he has made it plain that if Washington finds it useful to send an envoy to the Vatican, he must come as a representative of the Government with the confirmation of the Senate.

Advocates who argue that the appointment is not to a religious leader but to the ruler of the scrap of real estate called Vatican City do not get much support here. The mission is either to the Pope as the head of a worldwide church or it is nothing, it is pointed out; to pretend anything else is to make the appointment useless or reduce it to absurdity. All other countries sending representatives to the Vatican accredit them to the Holy See, and if the United States decides to send one at all it will follow the regular formula.

At present forty-six countries are listed in the Vatican. Some of the Embassies are now dormant—the iron curtain countries with the exception of representatives from the exiled Polish government, Guatemala and two or three small Latin-American states—but at least thirty-six are active. The latest to join the circle are Finland, Indonesia, India and Egypt. Arrangements are in process for sending representatives from Turkey and Pakistan. West Germany is about to renew relations and Japan intends to do so as soon as her independent status is established. Lebanon has a Minister and Syria and Iraq are expected to follow suit.* Yugoslavia withdrew her Minister after Tito took over, but through all the troubles with the church she has kept her Vatican Legation open with a secretary in charge.

On Christmas eve the whole diplomatic corps attends a midnight mass celebrated by the Pope in a private chapel in the Vatican. It is a strange and truly colorful congregation—the Ambassadors, Black, White, Yellow and Brown, wear full dress and yards of decorations, and the women long black gowns with lace mantillas. The number of Moslems is surprising and in general the variety of religious beliefs. Of the Big Powers only the United States, Russia and Communist China are unrepresented.

* The following now have representation: Pakistan, West Germany, Japan, Syria.

25

CHURCH AND STATE RELATIONS
IN SPAIN

February 11, 1952

The relation between church and state is the most complex of all the complexities of Spain. It is the prime example of the interplay of outward collaboration and inner conflict which makes this country so fascinating to explore and so hard to understand. Although a land of violent extremes, as the civil war demonstrated, it is the last place on earth that can be reported in terms of black and white. The first thing one learns in this mountain-walled and battle-scarred peninsula is that there is not one Spain but many and no generalization fits them all.

Officials speak of "relaxing controls and censorship" as economic strains ease and political passions cool. No one in the Government seriously pretends that it is not a dictatorship and no outside observer questions the adroitness of the head of the state in shifting his weight and playing one traditional force against another to preserve the balance he has managed to maintain for fourteeen years.

One vital difference between Spain and dictatorships of the East is that this country is open to the world. The Communists no sooner take over a nation than they lock the gates, whereas here the Bureau of Tourism works overtime to lure visitors in and make it easy for them to wander at will and talk freely with the assorted people they encounter.

There is also an important difference between Spain and the regimes of Hitler and Mussolini. This is not a one-party state. The Spanish version of Italian fascism and German national socialism, the Falange, is admittedly weaker today than it was a decade ago. This is partly because of the decisive defeat of fascism in World War II and partly because of the covert hostility of the two older and more powerful institutions—the church and the army.

The army is the main pillar of the regime. Franco has dismissed a number of generals and the armed forces are so poorly paid that even high ranking officers have to take on extra work to make a living. This is no less true of civil servants, whose wry boast is that Spain is a land of overemployment because every worker has at least two jobs. In spite of poverty, however, and the rivalries within the military ranks, there is general agreement even among his opponents that the army is 100 per cent loyal to the Generalissimo. There is equal agreement that no change of government is thinkable without the support of the army.

The church is an altogether different kind of force. It is difficult for any foreigner, Catholic or non-Catholic, to understand the unique position of the Catholic Church in Spain. In the first place it is the religion of the state, but unlike the established church in England or Sweden it is practically the one church in the country. Asked about opposition groups the other day, the Minister of Information remarked that Spain had 28,000,000 political parties, one for each inhabitant. The vast majority of these fiercely individual parties are at least nominal Catholics. They say of themselves that they are either more Catholic than the Pope or they are nothing.

The point is that all the divisions in this country are divisions among people of the same faith. This goes for the clergy as well as for the laity. There are priests in the underground resistance and in the Falange, Bishops who seem to ignore the lessons of the revolution, and others, like Bishop Herrera of Malaga, who heads a crusade for radical social reform. The most courageous critics of the Falange, notably Cardinal Segura of Seville, are to be found in the hierarchy, and the most Catholic province, the Basque country, is the most antagonistic to the regime.

The Spanish church as a whole, however, supports the Government. There are other reasons for this besides fear of communism and civil war. The latter is the powerful unlaid ghost that really governs Spain. The Republic disestablished the church and deprived it of its traditional privileges. The last year of the Republican regime was marked by a wave of religious persecution. Franco has restored the benefices of the clergy and religious teaching in the schools. He has rebuilt burned churches, established new seminaries, reopened and expanded charitable institutions.

But no church can flourish freely in a totalitarian state, even a Catholic church in a Catholic state. Sometimes openly, but oftener behind the scenes, the ecclesiastical authorities wage a struggle to preserve their independence. The nature of this struggle is suggested by the fact that certain pronouncements of the present Pope have been objectionable to the Spanish authorities. On at least one occasion a church paper was suppressed because it contained an editorial referring to a Papal utterance on the dangers of totalitarianism. Various reasons have deterred the Vatican from concluding a concordat with Spain, among them the question whether the state shall continue to have a voice in the nomination of Bishops.

Beyond all this, however, everything in Spain is associated with religion—history, art, the great days of exploration and missionary colonization. It is the most powerful of traditions in a country that lives on tradition. The Spaniard is passionately religious and passionately anti-religious, but in either case he is preoccupied with religion. This is a country in which the strange entity called the soul has reality, and it is a brash reporter who tries to evaluate it in political terms.

PART TWO

Spiritual Essays of Historical Significance

26

REMEMBERING ANOTHER
EASTER EVE IN GREECE

April 12, 1941

The mood of Good Friday is more appropriate to this week-end than the mood of Easter. The weight of the Cross was the weight of the sins of the world, and they never seemed heavier than in this dark week when what happened last year has happened all over again. Two more small nations have been savagely overrun for no reason except that they wished to preserve the irreducible minimum of independence within their own borders, and the "blitz" of the second Spring seems worse than the first just because it is a repetition.

It brings home that the strength of evil is not yet matched by the strength of resistance to evil. It rubs in the bitter truth that Hitler's power is in great part the weakness and unreadiness of his opponents. We are suffering from the ferocity of a revolution of destruction that sweeps over the earth in a hurricane of hate for all the things we prize. But in this penitential season it is good for our souls to realize that we are also paying the price for our own sins of sloth, complacency, selfishness and stupidity. By their power, wealth and freedom to act, the great democratic peoples were obligated to give a lead to the world, and their failure to do so before the forces of disorder broke loose puts upon them now the terrible responsibility of mobilizing every ounce of reserve energy they have to stop the avalanche and renew the foundations of order.

Of course, it can be done. One strong flame can light all the lamps again. On this Easter eve the thoughts of the writer go back to another Easter eve in Athens. In the spring dusk the whole city, so it seemed, crowded into the big square in front of the rather ugly modern cathedral. The overflow filled all the adjacent streets, block after block. The Greek Easter is celebrated thirteen days after that of the Western church, and it is celebrated more universally and more literally.

On Good Friday night an endless funeral procession moves through the city. Miles of mourners, carrying tapers and torches and chanting the deep, sonorous dirges of the Eastern ritual, follow the effigy of the dead Christ around Constitution Square, through the dark byways in the shadow of the Acropolis. They pass the big shops and the little whispering bazaars of Shoe Lane. In that place of the unburied past the candles sometimes cast a yellow glow on the columns of an ancient temple and illuminate that timeless quest of man for God which the stones of Greece suggest only less than the haunted hills of Palestine. Toward midnight the procession winds up the steep slopes of Lycabettus, a climbing line of flickering lights, to the sanctuary of St. George, a saint whose legend is as deeply embedded in Greek tradition as it is in the lore of England.

Easter is the great Greek holiday. For three days, in normal years, secular life is almost suspended while the people are absorbed in the drama of Calvary and Resurrection. The light is strangely clear in Greece, and that Easter Eve a pale radiance crowned the Parthenon long after the sea-colored twilight faded. The same phenomenon occurs at times on Mount Olympus. The cloud-swathed summit shines with an unearthly fire when the red plains of Macedonia are quite dark, and you see why to the old Greeks the tall peak was heaven, the abode of the gods, as to the Greeks fighting to-night for their lives in the shadow of that mountain it may seem more like hell, the encampment of devils.

We all carried candles to the square that night and waited, a hushed congregation of thousands, until a point of light sprang alive in the darkness. At the church door the Metropolitan of Athens had lighted the paschal candle. One of the priests lighted his candle from the first, and in no time the whole square flamed as one candle was ignited from another. Soon the path of light extended down every street, as far as the eye could see, and the cry, "Christ is Risen!" bursting from every throat, was as much like a shout of victory as if the Greeks were celebrating the triumph of their armies.

One remembers this scene because of the Greeks, to whom the Resurrection is as real and present as the events of today —and particularly because of those Greeks who came back from Asia Minor, refugees in the great post-war migration, and were settled in the country around Salonika, which the

Germans have now taken. Living for centuries among the Turks, their nationality was kept alive by their religion, and vice versa. Hardly rooted in the Macedonian soil, they are now refugees once more, and this tragedy within the larger tragedy wrings the heart of those who have witnessed their former sufferings and the heroism of the Greeks at home who made room for them in a poor and overcrowded land.

The people of Greece were as undaunted by that overwhelming problem of peace as they are by the terrors of unequal war. They are a very little people, a few million souls in all, perhaps too anxious to gather tonight to shout "Alleluia" because Christ is risen from the dead. Probably the roads around Athens are not filled this year with countrymen carrying lambs upon their shoulders. But the torch of faith and courage they hold aloft is like that single paschal candle from which all the other candles took their flame. They have lighted a light. That cannot be blacked out.

27

REFLECTIONS
IN TIME OF WAR

April 4, 1942

For nearly four years the world has followed the schedule of Adolf Hitler. The months and the seasons have been counted according to his timetable. The tempo of aggression has caused us all to move the clock ahead, to turn out the lights, to welcome Winter and dread Spring, to speed up the works of destruction and slow down the works of progress.

One little angry, brooding man has put the whole world on wartime. A man who could never keep step with anybody has forced millions of free and intelligent human beings to keep the time he sets. It's just as grotesque as the story of the Pied Piper or the fairy tale of the turnip that turned into a watch, but it is true that his clock has called the time not only for the peoples of Europe, not only for the confused leaders of the milling masses of India, summoned too suddenly to make terrible decisions, but for the incredulous people of the United States, jerked out of the safe isolation to face mortal danger in two oceans.

And then come Good Friday, and Easter, and the feast of the Passover. These feasts stem from more ancient festivals of pagan days that have celebrated from year to year and from century to century the annual miracle of the Spring. The recorded history of man is pretty short compared to the age of the earth and the aeons in which time is counted; but for 6,000 years there has never been an age so dark that the human spirit has not groped for symbols at this season to affirm its faith in the rebirth of life, in the resurrection of the dead, in the triumph of good over evil.

This year the white-bloused Greek shepherds are not carrying the newborn lambs on their shoulders through the gray olive groves of Amphyssa, as on one well-remembered Easter Eve. The Dalmatian peasants are not coming down from the hills, looking, in their bright embroideries, like a many-colored ribbon unwinding, to sing the Easter hymns in the village churches. Where are the people in Warsaw who crowded the steps of the cathedral shouting Easter greetings to the passers-by? Where are the Sicilians who danced in the big piazza in Palermo?

Only two years ago French boys in uniform paraded gayly with their girls in the sunlit avenues of the Bois. One of them bought a little tricolor boutonniere from a smiling vendor and presented it to the American with flourish. "Pour la victoire, madame!" he said, and everybody around took up the cry, "Pour la victoire!" Perhaps he thinks of it this Easter in a German prison camp.

Looking back on other Easters in many lands that now must live on Hitler's time, one knows with profound certainty that they do not believe in it. Better than the rest of us they know that it cannot displace the immemorial calendar that marks the vicissitudes of man. On this Easter, in the new unfolding of the timeless drama that leads from Calvary to the broken tomb on the dawn of the third day, they still live in hope.

America's first Easter on wartime is a reminder of the real basis of this hope. Americans are congenital optimists, extroverts and nonfatalists. They hope more fluently than any people on earth—perhaps because they have always been sure of the future. The disasters of the first four months of war are an unpleasant surprise. We are still blinking from the shock of discovering that the home front is literally "everywhere in the world." We are worried and confused and dismayed by the size of the conflict, but no American has the slightest doubt that we are going to win it. Any one who dips even superficially into the troubled cross-currents can testify that the thought of defeat simply does not enter the American imagination.

This confidence goes deeper than belief in the capacity of this country to out-produce all the Axis powers together when it gets going. This feeling is very strong, of course, especially among the producers, who are sure that by midsummer tanks and planes will be rolling off the assembly lines at a rate that cannot be duplicated anywhere. Stronger even than faith in American industrial power, however, is the prevailing instinct that this is a war against man himself, an assault upon the human race, and that humanity cannot be defeated.

A Yankee mechanic from Bridgeport expressed the common thought: "Hitler always reminds me of that crazy guy who built a hole in the sand and tried to pour the ocean into it," he said. "You just can't turn back the whole trend of human history. Here are the Filipinos fighting to be free, and the Indians insisting on running their own country. Do the Nazis believe that a throwback like Hitler can ever conquer anybody? Why, he's only stirring up more independence movements. He's fighting the human species, and the human species has never been licked. I figure that Hitler's time is short—and God's time is long."

That's the message of Easter. It is the eternal promise, annually renewed and always fulfilled in the end, of the victory of the human spirit.

28

THE TENUOUS LINK
BETWEEN TWO WORLDS

December 23, 1942

At Christmas time the thoughts of most adults go back over the years. They do not go back as far, perhaps, as the event which Christmas commemorates. Few think of the birth of Christianity in terms of the great ideological revolution that it was, or as the beginning of an era that has lasted to this day. The break-up of our world is more present just now in the minds of men than its continuity.

Yet Christmas is a sign of continuity, and in the middle of an upheaval that blots out the face of the future it is something to remember that through the wars and changes of 2,000 years we continue to tell time by the same calendar. For that means that under strains as great as the present, in dark lapses when cities crumbled and civilizations withered as they seem to do today, the connecting thread did not snap. In 1942 we are still bound to the first Anno Domini, and through that to the older chronology of which the new is only the continuation.

There is no break in the serial story. But when most of us look back at Christmas, it is not down the highways of history that we gaze but down the narrow paths of personal experience. Christmas is the grown-up's link with childhood. It is a repetitious day, full of echoes, and so much the same from place to place and from year to year that it lights up the changes that have occurred in environment, circumstances, human relations, the texture and the tone of life.

Also, and above all this year, it lights up the changes that have taken place in the world. For while Christmas memories are mostly personal, they are so tangled up with the memories and traditions of the human race that at some point the narrow path touches the broad highway, and the individual is swept into the stream of universal experience.

This is particularly true this Christmas, because in the immediate background of the restrictions and sacrifices that make the war real to Americans looms a picture of suffering more cruel and widespread than the world has ever known. As yet our deprivations are mere discomforts, and it is impossible even to imagine what war, looting, occupation and forced labor have done to almost the entire population of the European Continent. A letter received a few weeks ago from a friend in a neutral country, written in French, ended on a note of despair. "If I could write freely and in the clearest English," it said, "I could find no words which would make anybody in your world understand what is happening in mine. You live in another atmosphere, and you cannot realize how continued hunger, darkness and terror poison the air and shrivel the soul when the victims aren't groups or individuals but whole nations."

The testimony of those who come out of Europe or are in close touch with what goes on inside adds up to a searching and important question: Are we thinking in the same terms as the peoples we are fighting to liberate? The French, for instance, are they as much concerned over the future of their empire, over the possible political consequences of our recognition of Darlan, as they are over where the next meal is coming from?

Scarcity of food, increased by the loss of a dribble of supplies from North Africa, has become so serious that the black market is almost the only market, except for bread, and inflation has reached a point where buying on the black market cannot be done out of wages or income but only out of what's left of the capital of the once well-to-do. Getting food is almost an occupation in France. It is the preoccupation of Italy. It is hardly too much to say that the occupied countries, including all but the armies and the ruling cabal in Germany and their henchmen, are so absorbed in the daily struggle against physical hunger that even the hunger for freedom, except in the most valiant spirits, is secondary. The energy for rebellion runs low in such conditions. The miracle is that among the Greeks and the Poles, who have endured the most unspeakable torments, the flame of resistance still burns. It flares up here and there in every land, oftener than we know, but the apathy of semi-starvation spreads, too, and creates an indifference to our talk of tomorrow that we should not forget.

The outside world, living on a different plane, breathing a different air, speaks a language that is difficult to translate into the narrowing limits of European speech. One must wonder sometimes if most of the short-wave messages we pour into the Continent have any relation to the realities of their situation.

Nations cannot go through the experience of these years and come out the same. The liberating forces will go into a Europe that is changed, that cannot be fully known to any outsider, even those who have kept in the closest connection with the inside. We know it will be hungry, stripped, proletarianized, but not what thoughts the people will be thinking, not what forces will eventually push to the top. But we know, too, that nations do not die. The fact that Christmas is still with us, 1,942 years after, gives a certain confidence that the thread that connects the present with the past and the future cannot be wholly broken even now.

29

ON SAVING THE FRUITS
OF OUR CIVILIZATION

October 9, 1943

If the letters received by the writer during the last few days are an index, a great many oddly assorted Americans are deeply stirred and worried by the fate that hangs over Rome. Apparently there is real concern in this country for the artistic treasures of Italy. Some write in sorrow, like the up-State farmer who says that "the thought of Rome destroyed hangs heavily on the heart of millions of people like me that you will never hear from." Some write in anger, like the Boston professor of the classics who protests against the "feeble attitude of resignation which accepts this outrage against our civilization as if it were merely an Italian loss, or as if we are capable of doing nothing to prevent it."

The letters cover a wide area of space and opinion. They

come from a soldier in a Midwest training camp, from a woman worker in a Jersey munitions plant, from teachers and business men. A Bishop grieves over the peril to religious monuments, particularly the ancient shrines built above the Catacombs and connected with the memory of the early Apostles.

But most of the correspondents are thinking more of the other Rome—the museum of Western culture. They echo the complaint of an art lover of Charlottesville, Va., who says that he awaits news of the possible destruction of the art works of civilization in Italy with dread. "I do not agree with your seeming to sit quiet and let our leaders decide which is the right way to handle these priceless possessions. It is true that we must save civilization, but what about taking forethought to save the fruits of civilization? AMG talks about 'throwing a cordon about the remains.' Are we to attempt nothing to save things whole?"

This correspondent is particularly worried about Florence, the unique flower of one great epoch—the Renaissance —as Rome is the mélange of all the epochs of our era. By the will of the last and one of the greatest of the Medicis, Anna Maria Ludovica, the vast possessions of her family were left to the state of Tuscany, on condition that none of them should be removed and all should be the inheritance of the people of Florence, to be held in trust by them "for the benefit and free enjoyment of the peoples of all nations."

The gentleman from Virginia reminds us of this legacy of ours, which the Florentines have faithfully preserved and administered. His suggestion is that as co-owners of the wealth of palaces, paintings, sculptures, books, manuscripts, gems and other treasure we publish to the Nazis and the world that the Allied Governments reaffirm the "will" of Anna Maria

Ludovica; declare that so far as we are concerned Florence
will be an "open city" which we shall neither shell nor bomb;
reappoint the citizens of Florence as guardians of these treasures in behalf of all civilized peoples, and, to insure them
against destruction or theft, announce that we shall hold responsible a list of persons who are named.

This "beau geste" certainly would be good propaganda,
though nothing in the record of the Nazis offers any reason
to hope that they would pay the slightest attention to such a
proclamation or that they will not proceed with the spolia-
tion of Florence and of Rome. In Naples they have left
nothing they could take away, not only works of art but machinery, furniture, copper kettles and pans.

They have left behind time bombs, like the one that blew
up the magnificent modern postoffice, pride of the Fascist era,
with everybody in it. They have left behind a trail of hatred
as searing as the scorched earth policy they are pursuing.
They are behaving in Italy as they have not before behaved
in the west, with a ferocity explicable only on the ground
that they are bent on ruining what they know they have lost.
If they did not feel hate for Italy and the hate of Italy, if they
had not given it up, they might be expected to spare Rome
and Florence if only to blow up the empty power of Mussolini. For of what use are the puppets to the Germans if their
only role is to participate in the savage destruction of the life
and treasures of their country?

The Nazis are crazed by frustration. If their retreat across
Europe is marked by the rage for destruction they show in
Italy, they will pile up undying hostility. This is unlike the
policy of the military leaders; in defeat they always think of
the future of Germany. But it opens the door wide for us to
think of the future and point at the contrast between their

ways and ours. We would be wise to take bold risks if thereby we could prevent the Germans from destroying what it is our first interest to save. Our business is to foil their desperate plot to bring the walls of the temple down with them. There can be no doubt that the American people's conception of victory is to save everything in Europe that we can.

30

WHERE THE CHRISTMAS LIGHTS
ARE OUT

December 25, 1943

The fifth Christmas of the war finds a large part of the civilized world exhausted, ravaged, crazed or dulled by cruelty.
The "countless thousands" who suffered from man's inhu-
manity to man in the past have multiplied into countless millions in the present. The horror has become so vast that it is
almost impersonal. Individual agony is all but lost sight of in
the wholesale atrocities practiced by Nazi terror squads—men
trained for terror—in occupied territory, particularly in the
East. When cities are bombed the scurrying inhabitants are
only incidental wreckage in the destruction of rails and stores
and forges. When children slowly starve, unable to hold out
until the rescue expeditions arrive, they are hardly more than
fading shadows in a dark and faceless landscape.

The President spoke yesterday of our "unseen allies" and indeed nobody can see far enough to see their faces. Nobody has a mind big enough to understand their thoughts or a heart wide enough to feel their misery. But Christmas brings it close again for the traveler who looks from this safety zone on the shattered settings of many Christmases.

Christmas is a haunted time when the scenes of yesterday blur the picture of today. There is the English village where the waits sang carols in lighted doorways of the old timbered cottages or the pleasant London square where the fog swept through the windows on Christmas night and added its own touch of mystery to the tree, the children's wonder and the sense of insulated security the English always felt in their snug and misty island. Village and city square live only in memory; the first bombs that fell on Britain wiped out both. The little church in Naples where the sailors crowded wide-eyed around the ancient "Presepio" is part of the wreckage of the waterfront. In Bethlehem itself the shrine that covers the cave of the Nativity is encircled by Army trucks and armored cars.

Moscow is grimmer than it was on a grim Christmas ten years ago. The dim old cathedral at Kiev filled on the Russian Christmas with the imploring, quavering voices of the old is a skeleton in a skeleton city. This year the hotel waiters will not sneak in for a stolen glimpse of the American Christmas tree, crossing themselves instinctively at the sight of the candles and the angels. If they are still alive they can have a Christmas tree of their own even on the battlefield.

Little is left of the old square where the Christmas market of Nuremberg was held. The tinkling toys and gingerbread men dance no more in the rainbow light cast on the snow by the stained-glass windows of the medieval church. Mines are being laid to blow up the little piazza in Rome where the children preached on Christmas afternoon. Hungry ghosts walk in Ship Lane and the Street of the Coppersmiths in Athens, once filled with Christmas bustle, bargaining and laughter. The wide promenade of the Champs-Elysées, where the tight little family circles of Paris paraded primly after Christmas dinner is now the exercise ground of the German garrison.

Nothing is as it was save Christmas itself. The shattered frames of memory's pictures are the settings of human life. They help the mind to realize the broken homes, the lost traditions, the physical degradation and moral torture human beings are enduring. At the same time we know that in places where the walls are crumbled and the lights are out Christmas will still be kept because it has to be, because it repeats year after year the one affirmation man must believe in if he is to keep on struggling.

The story of Christmas is the story of the importance of man. The idea embodied in the Child born in the manger of Bethlehem is the idea of the supreme importance of the redemption of the human race. It was the incarnation in the Western World, the world of the Roman Empire, of the old Hebraic faith in the immeasurable value of the human soul.

This is the idea humanity is still fighting for. Not since the beginning of the Christian era has it been so furiously assailed and so fiercely defended as it is today. For what is the naked issue of the most universal war in history but the right of man to be himself? Other issues complicate and confuse the minds of armies and nations. The fundamental antithesis is often blunted. The systems representing self-government in the most advanced form it has yet attained are fighting with one great totalitarian system against another. But underneath the mixed motives, the extreme nationalisms, the non-syn-chronizing conceptions of government and life that are fused in the great coalition runs a common will to resist conquest and dominion, to retain at any cost the right of nations and eventually of individuals to work out their own salvation in their own way.

No lesser aim could justify the horrors of this war. The memories and the thoughts that assail us at Christmas time could not be borne unless somewhere in the depths of the human spirit there is a core of faith that the great symbolism of the Nativity is true. The Child was homeless, too. He es-caped the slaughter of the innocents only by a flight into exile. He was stoned in the highways and hanged on a cross. Yet the idea lived because the spirit of man is stronger than the walls he builds or the ruin he works when he vainly seeks to destroy himself and enslave himself.

31

EASTER IN THE FIFTH YEAR
OF THE WAR

April 8, 1944

Reporters in Jerusalem think it worth while to cable that the tension of the last few weeks abates in Palestine as Christians, Jews and Mohammedans turn to the observance of their great spring festivals. This is a small item of news to set beside the stories of three-dimensional battles raging without pause from the Ukraine to the South Pacific. It does not signify a truce even in such marginal struggles as are waged in Palestine.

There is no truce on this fifth Easter of the war; there will be no truce anywhere until it is won. The spring breaks after a winter of incessant but still inconclusive fighting, although the most cursory comparison of the positions of both sides today with that of last October shows what a momentous winter it has been. It does not break on a prospect of peace, but on a stage set for bigger military action. The whole world is waiting with taut nerves for the test to which every action up to now has been directed.

This waiting itself is a test. In a time of tremendous movement the intervals of suspense are as trying, perhaps more so, as the crescendoes of action. Reporters back from the front say that low morale is to be found only in troops waiting behind the lines; in the fighting ranks the spirit is high. For the civilian in this country, very remote indeed from the actual experience of war, vigils like this are an even harder test of temper and of purpose. They are times when he must turn in upon himself to find the reasons for endurance and for faith in his cause. This struggle comes down in the end through all the military and political hierarchies to the individual will. A civil war within a world war, it is a personal war within both, fought at last in private, so to speak, on that moral plane where each man battles with himself.

In the first issue of Tricolor, the American edition of La France Libre, published in London after the fall of France and later distributed in the French underground, the leading article deals with the effects of four years of excommunication from the world on the mind of France. It asks the questions on which the future turns: What has happened to the people living cut off from the free world? Will the unity of Western civilization be threatened because for so many years Americans and Europeans have been separated? Or, when the silence is broken, will the enslaved surprise the free? "It may well turn out," the editor answers, "that France will repay her liberators not in kind but in the fruits of silence—the thinking on which the new world will be founded."

The fruits of the silent war may have as important an influence on the future as the results of the active fighting. But this silent struggle goes on not in occupied Europe alone but alongside and behind the battle in every country at war. Under the feverish activity of the production centers, the training camps, the ports, the supply lines, people are making decisions in their own minds that will determine the shape of victory. They are deciding what is coming out of this agony. They are either winning the fight for liberty or giving it up. They are determining whether the world is going back to the anarchy which was the pre-condition of this war, and will be the sure road to the next, or whether we care enough for security and order to fight for it, against setbacks and disillusionments, as hard as we fight for military victory.

These decisions will be made in the minds of men. Actually, they are made in the soul, for they are fundamentally moral and spiritual decisions. Germany lacks power to defeat the coalition of power ranged against her. Our real peril is that for want of thought, for want of a true appraisal of the issues, we shall defeat ourselves by abandoning the purpose for which we fight. This purpose is, first, to preserve our own liberties and the chance to develop and adapt them to new needs in our own way, and, second, to create a world in which free peoples can live and develop—a world where power is pooled and curbed to insure long periods of peace. But these aims are not national but individual in the sense that no nation can pursue them unless the individual citizens are resolved to continue the war for peace long after the enemy lays down his arms.

These reflections are not so remote as they seem from the Easter scene in Palestine. It is not mere coincidence that these days are holy days, the most solemn of the year, for Christians, Jews and Moslems. It is not fortuitous that one little strip of ground on the Mediterranean littoral is the Holy Land for three great religions that have profoundly influenced the world. It is not strange that on the occasions when they are most themselves, at once separate and united, they pray together at the Mosque and the Temple and the Church of the Holy Sepulchre.

Actually it is a meeting place, and a meeting place it will remain.

Somewhere in this manifestation is the dim assurance that men who believe in something can get together on that bedrock basis even when they are divided on more superficial issues. Anyway, Easter is not a feast of hope but a feast of faith. It affirms the triumph of life over death, just as Jerusalem as a meeting place proves the endless power of ideas to possess people and influence life. In this time of suspense before the great battle is this a promise or a warning that Americans will win out of it the kind of victory they believe in and are determined to achieve? In the end can the fruits of action be other than the fruits of silence?

32

HOPES AND FEARS ON
THE FIRST PEACETIME EASTER

April 20, 1946

This is the first peacetime Easter in seven years. Last Easter we were still fighting in Europe and Asia. V-E Day was not celebrated until May 8 and V-J Day until nearly four months later.

The face of victory is darkened with terrible shadows this Easter. No one expected the end of war to bring peace. But no one foresaw the trail of ruin and human disintegration the conflict would leave behind it. No one thought that peace would be so hard to make that the terms of the first settlement could not be agreed on a year after Germany's collapse.

Unconditional surrender made the victors absolute masters of the situation. They do not have to negotiate with the enemy. They command force and resources to do anything they like with the world. It is fair to say that they have not quarreled over the division of the spoils and have voluntarily decided to support a collective security system. The nature of the frictions in the Security Council proves that the members take it seriously. There is not the slightest indication that Russia or any other nation has any intention of breaking away from this resounding international forum.

The chief trouble is that only the Great Powers can establish the conditions of peace, and they are not in accord on what these conditions are. Their discord creates the atmosphere in which we live. It explains why men are losing confidence not only in their leadership but in peace itself.

It is Easter, and the human race hungers for signs of Resurrection as it hungers for bread. The war is over, and want and misery and discord continue to haunt the earth. And worse than widespread want is widespread fear, the fear that there will be no peace.

But that is not the whole picture. We have won a war that might have been lost. The guns are quiet and the birds sing. In every land it is a spring of peculiar brightness and beauty, as if nature were doing her utmost to camouflage the scars. From Rome and Athens, Brussels and London, come reports of sunny skies, of flowers abloom again in the public gardens, of people parading in streets and parks celebrating the end of the bitterest winter in history with the same sense of deliverance they felt when the shooting stopped. Even the pale and tattered people of Vienna and Budapest are thawing out in the sun. Cologne and Essen must be ghastlier in the spring light than they were in the gray fogs of winter, but the German countryside is green and tranquil and new leafage will cover the gaps in the denuded woods.

The Russians love Easter above all feasts, partly because they celebrated it with such pomp and color in the old days, partly because their winters are so hard and dark. It is the great church holiday, and this year more people are going to church in Moscow than since before the revolution. There is a rumor that the church bells will ring once more. If their deep bass clangor, different enough from all other bells to be the voice of Russia itself, breaks upon the air it will stir thousand-year-old instincts and emotions that two or three decades of silence have not been enough to efface.

The old walled city of Jerusalem is a symbol of the world in its present state of suspense. The tensions in Jerusalem are perhaps nearer the breaking point than conflicts anywhere else. The only antagonism stronger than the contest between Arabs and Zionists for that passionately disputed land is the anger of both against the British. Yet the feast of the Passover and the devotions of Holy Week were observed with more fervor by greater numbers than for many years. In the setting of an armed camp, with guards massed at every corner, the pilgrims thronged the Via Dolorosa or flocked to the Temple—and perhaps to the Mosque of Omar, for devotion is contagious—in a procession one spectator describes as "a pageant of piety and peace."

The first post-war winter has made it starkly clear that if people want peace they have to pay dearly for it, with sweat and tears if not with blood. They are learning that the worst threat to peace is starvation, and that the first defense of this nation, and the first responsibility of the United Nations, is to give this "situation" priority over every political dispute, and deal with it as a world problem. U. N. cannot begin to build order on skeletons, to the accompaniment of hunger riots and mob violence, and it will lose the confidence of mankind unless it deals with this elemental and frontierless "disturbance of the peace."

The hungry are kept alive by hope, and Easter is the feast of hope, of life triumphing over death, of the flower breaking through the mold, of the unconquerable human spirit, forever ready to begin anew. Hope is one of the commonest blossoms of the spring. It grows wild in the crannies of Europe's ruins. This country is the source and spring of that hope; and as Americans learn that the dearest commodity on earth is peace, and that out of their riches they have to foot a good part of the bill, they must see they can no longer afford the luxury of political irresponsibles and moral isolationists. America has arrived at the place and the moment when the desperate hopes of the world are in her keeping. It is in our power, if we use it, to justify the hopes—or the fears.

33

THE WAR ON THE SIDE
OF THE ANGELS

April 5, 1947

This is Holy Week for Christians and Jews. More people of all denominations attend religious services during these days than at any other time of the year. Human society has made as many revolutions through the centuries as the irreversible wheel of time. Twice in this century the world has turned upside down and come back with historic landmarks shattered and the weights shifted that hold the political structure in balance. The tempo of change is so speeded up in this generation that the old surprises us much more than the new.

The crowded churches of Holy Week are a startling proof of the enduring hold of tradition, ritual and belief. In the Passover and the Paschal seasons the same events are commemorated year after year with the same ceremonial by the two great religions of the Western world—or the one great religion, for the Old Testament and the New are two chapters of one Bible. Both came out of the Middle East, that strange, germinal desert which today, as always, is the plexus of the earth, and together they constitute the Book that more than any other has given its moral content and its deistic character to Western civilization.

The events these days recall were local happenings in a small world. Even in that small world they were small incidents, as unimportant to the powers of their time as were the Jews who followed Moses out of Egypt or the Jewish disciples who founded a new church on the riven tomb of Christ. Compared to the Punic Wars, the discovery of America, the French and Russian Revolutions, the two world upheavals we have witnessed, they were mere ripples in the stream of history. Yet the stream carries them on. They have outlasted the revolutions of two eras, the rise and fall of empires, the sweep of changes that have altered the habits, the folkways and the environment of human life.

They survive because they are remembered by millions of people. Even those who have forgotten live under laws shaped by the Ten Commandments and social compulsions emanating from the Sermon on the Mount. What we call "the West" is not so much a geographic as a religious conception; it is a culture, a system of values, a principle of development, an emphasis on the person, growing out of the Judaeo-Christian teaching and tradition.

This spiritual tradition is what is challenged by communism. The conflict between the so-called "East" and the so-called "West" is political, economic, ideological, but fundamentally it is religious—the totalitarian religion that man is the creature of the state against the religion of individual free will and responsibility. The war marked a kind of climax of human suffering, and suffering is supposed to impel men to turn to religion. Whether the losses of yesterday, the misery of today and the uncertainty of tomorrow are producing a religious revival is a question difficult to answer. There is evidence on both sides. In Europe the churches are certainly more crowded than before, not only in countries where many churches are destroyed, as in England, Germany, Austria and Italy, but also in Paris, Rome, Prague and Edinburgh, where they are numerous and undamaged. An American who spent last Easter in Moscow reports that the people swarmed to the churches in such numbers that those who could not get in literally hung on to the outside walls.

All accounts indicate that there is a tremendous revival of religious observance in Russia since the Orthodox Church was recognized by the Government. This proves that religion does not die, but the recognition of the church does not mark a change in the attitude of the Soviet leaders. Communist doctrine remains frankly anti-religious.

On the other side, disorientation and hopelessness have produced a wave of nihilism among the youth of Germany and other defeated countries. Among European youth generally, for that matter, there is a tendency either to believe in nothing or to accept Communist dogma, which is preached everywhere among the very young with zeal and a kind of angry fervor that has its appeal. If it were not for the Red Army and the return of broken-down prisoners of war, they might have won the young of Europe by now. As it is, they have to fight complete skepticism on one side and a conservative and religious reaction on the other.

It cannot be said that the religious tradition unifies. There is no "religious front." Nor does the conscience of the Western world develop any great surge of moral indignation against the slavery, terrorism and cruelty that have followed the war like a plague. Monstrous things are happening to human beings on both sides of the Iron Curtain. Behind the Easter parades and the crowded houses of worship—too far behind to be seen and never to be imagined—are legions of almost dehumanized people, in labor camps, internment camps, outcasts from every camp, victims of war, persecution and so-called peace treaties.

Yet there is a Western civilization, based on spiritual virtues even when it does not practice them, and it is this that freedom-loving people are beginning to rise out of their callousness and confusion to value and defend. The clearer the issues become in this struggle, the more apparent it is that they can never be answered by war, but only by a reaffirmation and demonstration of respect for the God-given rights of man. The side of the angels always wins in the end.

34

EASTER REFLECTIONS
IN A TIME OF DECISION

March 27, 1948

The dark uncertainties of the times will not prevent a large segment of the human race from celebrating Easter. Easter is the feast of hope, of the triumph of the spirit over death and defeat, and that is what millions of bewildered people want to think of in these days. They are hungrier for hope than for bread. They turn with relief from the panorama called the world, so thickly strewn with man-made trouble spots, to the earth itself, which can always be depended on to blossom out at this season with a burst of new life, as fresh as if each year were the first spring. With faith or doubt, some turn to heaven, drawn by the thought that somewhere there must be a world as well ordered and reliable as the visible creation.

The Fifth Avenue parade may be unique in its careless

opulence, but in London, Paris, Rome, Athens, Prague, if the day is bright, streets and parks will be filled with similar crowds, all dressed up in the best they have and equally bent on making the most of a holiday. The Easter outing is more real than any political demonstration. In the Luxembourg Gardens, as in Central Park, it is mostly made up of little family parties, merged together in the observance of a common festival, and in this community people are more themselves than when they separate into parties, sects or classes.

This year the parade is perhaps more meaningful than usual. Now more than ever people seem anxious to cling to the customary. In Western Europe, at least, they never appeared so determined to maintain the appearance of normality, to go through the motions of normal living. Never were they so jealous of their habits and traditions. One hears more of "Western Culture" than ever before.

The churches are unwontedly crowded. So are the public gardens. It is almost impossible to get a seat for a concert. Extraordinary art exhibits travel from city to city and the throngs pushing into the museums are so great that the masterpieces are nearly invisible. These manifestations may or may not indicate a great religious revival or an increased popular interest in nature or the arts. They do express a quickened sense of the value of the civilization that is felt to be in danger.

This feeling is widespread and instinctive. In a queue in front of a Paris bank when 5,000-franc notes were being turned in, a workman in faded blue overalls passed the time studying the sculptured façade of a famous old church across the street. As the line moved up he said to his companion: "It's worth something to live in a country that has been civilized so long." When Togliatti, the Communist leader, wants to flatter the Roman masses, he does better with talk of the glories of the Roman past than with Marxist arguments.

The Europe we are trying to strengthen needs to believe in itself. It needs the stimulant of hope and self-confidence quite as much as material help. Americans will delude themselves if they imagine that the Recovery Program for Europe or the military measures by which we propose to fortify ourselves will be enough to win the tremendous contest we are now engaged in.

By their infiltration into every country and their complete disregard of rules, truth and human feeling, the Communists have weapons we cannot match. But we have moral weapons which they cannot match, which they would not know how to use if they could, and the sooner we mobilize our moral forces and appeal to Europe to join us in saving the virtues as well as the values of our civilzation—honor, truth, self-respect, compassion—the more effective will be the material and military defenses we are setting up.

Europe trembles because it is physically weak and dependent on outside help. It is terrified by talk of war because it sees itself as the battleground. As a matter of fact, although fear of war colors the thought of every European nation, there is less talk about it over there than here at home. That is partly because this country has to take the responsibility for action. It is faced with decisions, evidently sudden decisions, which require that the American people should be aroused to a sense of danger. But is it impossible to take the steps common prudence dictates quietly and calmly?

Obviously we are acting to prevent a miscalculated move that would lead to war. We have to safeguard ourselves in the first place, and as a great Power we have to safeguard the world. But the more we prepare for war, the more we are obligated to keep the emphasis on peace and redouble our efforts to construct the framework and conditions of peace. It is hard for Americans to keep an even keel and an even temper, but the time has come when it is quite as incumbent on us to be steady as to be strong. The issues are in our hands; we create the moral atmosphere of the world.

Even to carry out the Marshall Plan, Europe needs the Easter hope of resurrection and peace. With hope it can build, with hope it can rise and march, with hope it can win a great war without bombs or armies. But only this country can cast out the fear that corrodes the spring, and it cannot do this without rising to heights of courage, wisdom and confidence of which we have never dreamed ourselves capable.

35

IF STALIN COULD REVIEW
NEW YORK'S EASTER PARADE

April 18, 1949

The old lady was in a worn black coat, but she had a new hat with a wreath of red roses around the crown and two corsages of red roses pinned to her shoulder. She was wedged in between two pretty granddaughters, in gray suits just out of the bandboxes, on the steps of St. Patrick's Cathedral as the biggest Easter Parade in history jammed the Avenue. She couldn't move, and didn't want to, for from her vantage point she could look down on the preening crowds that packed the adjoining blocks from wall to wall, so closely that buses and automobiles were shooed out of the way and people could move only in slow waves and eddies, with the effect of a flower garden in the wind.

The garden effect came from the hats. There were miles

of flowered hats, it seemed; never were so many piled into one place, at any rate; they bloomed and criss-crossed in a multi-colored profusion that made the lilies and fountains in Rockefeller Plaza appear tame and sober. It was a gigantic display of new hats—or, some one remarked, like the free-enterprise system showing off. For this was a dress parade not of the few but of the million. It was a parade in which there were no spectators because all were participants.

The girls under the hats were of all ages and all types, but whether they stepped decorously out of St. Thomas's, swarmed up from the lower East Side, or were visitors from other towns, they looked oddly alike. They looked alike, "standardized" if you like, because you could not distinguish the rich from the poor; they were all dressed up in the latest styles and they were pleased with themselves and what they saw. Compared to any other crowd in the world this Easter, they appeared happy, carefree and opulent.

The old lady with the roses on her hat was not opulent. When she tried to anchor her corsages, her hands showed the scars of hard work. Like many in the throngs she watched with such lively satisfaction, she was an immigrant in the long past and the rhythms of the County Kerry still sang in her speech. But she was not thinking of Ireland, or that on this Easter, anniversary of the Easter rising of 1916, the last tie with the British crown is broken and the Free State becomes in name what it has been in fact for years, an independent republic.

She was thinking of America. "It's a grand sight," she said once, "so many people in all their finery." And later: "I wish he could see it." "Grandpa?" one of the girls murmured sympathetically, in the accents of an East Side finishing school. "No, not grandpa," said the old lady, impatiently. "He has better sights to see. I mean that old Stalin."

But Fifth Avenue on Easter Sunday would probably irritate Stalin even more than he is already exasperated with the United States. Moscow is planning to build better skyscrapers than New York's, but they are still on paper. It promises to open superior shops stocked with enough clothes for everybody and that everybody can buy. But mass production for the masses is the invention of the capitalist system; so far it has not been attained by the Soviet state. At the present rate it will take a long series of five-year plans before the Soviet woman can buy a dress, a hat or a pair of shoes for anything near the price the average New York working girl paid for her Easter outfit.

It would not be surprising if Stalin is more annoyed by the Easter dress parade than by Wall Street. The distribution of wealth in this country is far from equable or general, but it is wider than anywhere else on earth, and the distribution more than the accumulation irks the Soviet leaders because it underlines the pregnant fact that there is no communism in the Marxist sense in the Soviet Union and no capitalism in the United States as it was conceived in *Das Kapital*.

The two systems that oppose each other under the old names have developed into something quite different. Communism, which was to cause the withering of the state, has brought about the most despotic state in history. And capitalism, supposed to concentrate all wealth and ownership in a few hands, has turned into a mass-production system providing goods for the greatest number of people. "By their fruits ye shall know them," and by their fruits the well-read man from Mars would certainly decide that the American system was approaching what he thought was communism while the Soviet system fitted into his concept of capitalism— the subjugation of the many to the interests of a few all-powerful individuals.

This must be Stalin's great grievance against this country. He is a logical man, who has studied and interpreted Marx and Lenin with enormous diligence, and is too faithful to their gospel and too enclosed in his own world to understand that both capitalism and democratic socialism have been molded by events into something quite different from the rigid imperatives which shape his outlook. It is more accurate to say they have been molded by people, for it is human forces, people moving, thinking, aspiring, experimenting, that work changes in the systems under which they live. This is why democracies grow, evolve and win by persuasion, while systems in which people have no voice remain sterile and can conquer only by force.

36

AND THE STAR OF BETHLEHEM
STILL SHINES

December 24, 1949

Early in the century a French politician boasted that he
would put out the Star of Bethlehem.* This year, in Moscow,
they launch the annual campaign against Christmas and
claim that the Red Star is now the light of the world. Yet today the name of Viviani is almost forgotten in France and
thirty-odd crusades are not enough to make the Russian
people forget Christmas. One remembers a Christmas in
Moscow in the Thirties when an American lighted a tiny
tree in a hotel room and set a golden star and a pink angel
on top. All day long the place was filled with the maids and
waiters of the Soviet staff, who sneaked in like home-sick

---

* Presumably this refers to the suppression of religious orders in France, 1902
and The Associations Law, 1905 enacted under Premier Combes.

children to cross themselves, sometimes with tears, before that symbol of the past.

Plucked from the skies a thousand times, the Star of Bethlehem continues to shine. The little town to which it guided the Wise Men of the East on the first Christmas is again, this year as last, closed to all but a few pilgrims. The birthplace of Christ is behind the Arab lines in the divided Holy Land and visitors have to get permits to make the journey, the diplomats who motor down the high road from Jerusalem as well as the lesser folk who take the rough round-about trail over the hills. But people will go none the less. The Church of the Nativity will be filled tonight with chants and incense and crowds pushing down the steps hewn out of the rock, worn into grooves by the feet of the endless multitudes who have sought "heaven in a cave, and in a manger, God."

And everywhere else, this season, people are remembering —their childhood, old customs, old friends, the stars they once followed, the friendless and the poor. For a few bright days, while New York is a garden of Christmas trees, while chimes play "Come All Ye Faithful" in the sparking dusk, while the streets are jammed with shoppers laden with green and red packages, the big, impersonal town becomes something like a vast, bustling family, everbody thinking of somebody else, jostled to a jelly but warmed and humanized by the impulse to give and the common search for gifts.

To one who has not been here at this season since the war years the sheer lavishness of New York at Christmas time is startling. Everything comes in piles, it seems—scarfs, neckties, jewels, furs, bags, perfumes, dolls, mechanized toys. The quantity and variety of the display in grocers' windows exercise an endless fascination on those who for years have seen food rationed and queued-up for. After the dim cities of the post-war world, the lights, walls and rivers and trees of light are blinding. The curdled-up traffic is a caricature of movement and opulence.

The Christmas shopping spree is not confined to New York, however. Despite Britain's dollar shortage, perhaps because of it, more money has been spent in London during the holidays than in any year since the war. For the first time the shops are full of goods, even luxury goods, and so far the devaluation has not noticeably increased domestic prices. A letter from a London friend reports that austerity has gone by the board and that for the first time in a decade the British are enjoying a "fat, jolly, old-fashioned Christmas, complete with waits, holly, roast goose and plum pudding."

The Parisians have always had more to buy than the Londoners. All luxuries are available at a price in France, but the change there is that those who have money are buying at any price. The traditional French thrift is disappearing, and although this is a sign of inner uncertainty—"eat, drink and be merry, for tomorrow we die"—it gives a varnish of gaiety and luxury to the surface that makes France appear unusually festive this year.

In Rome emphasis is on the religious rather than the secular significance of Christmas, particularly at this solemn opening of the Holy Year, when the Eternal City resumes its ancient primacy as the capital of Christendom. Italy is poorer than France or England, but it is gayer by temperament, and the Italian taste and flair for "festa" helps them to forget their nagging problems while they celebrate. Even the Western Germans are so much better off, relatively, than they have been for years that the first time since 1940, when austerity was already the rule, they are observing their favorite holiday.

Throughout the Western world, indeed, Christmas is being kept with a special, an almost passionate, zest. And with a resurgence of religious feeling. "There's a run on religious cards this year," said a harassed bookseller who had stocked up on fat Santas and snowy landscapes. People are throwing themselves into the celebration of this festival of birth, the most human and touching of holy days, to shut out for a blessed interval the shadows of war and cruelty, frustration and fear, in which they live.

In these days more than ever, perhaps, man wants to believe in the mystery of Bethlehem, in the miracle of the Messiah coming to share his lot and save him from the fate he has invented for himself. Perhaps the spectacle of the deification of Stalin causes a world nourished in its youth on Tables of the Law and the great Scriptures of the Old and New Testaments to turn with relief to the story of the Child born in a manger who went forth with nothing but a staff and a scrip to preach mercy and peace. In the baleful effulgence of the Red Star, perhaps he seizes upon this day to remind himself that the Star of Bethlehem still shines.

37

THE RINGING MESSAGE
OF THE EASTER BELLS

April 8, 1950

Twenty years ago, when tours to the Soviet Union were the fashion, Moscow was still the city of churches and church bells. Even more than Rome, the Sunday morning air of the capital of the revolution was shaken by the hoarse clangor of rusty and remembering chimes. Visitors in Moscow on Easter Eve could hear the great bell of the Kremlin, mother bell of Russia, sound the deep note that released all the others.

In Athens the paschal candle of the Archbishop supplies the light for every other candle, and as the flame passes from hand to hand in the Cathedral Square it weaves a pattern that spreads in no time through the streets and up the slopes of Lycabettus. For a moment, in that glow of Christian faith, the temples of the Acropolis look dark and lonely.

In Moscow it was the Kremlin bell that started the alleluias. A dozen years after the revolution the midnight chime was still repeating its immemorial message to the people. A story was current in those days that the sound broke up a meeting of the Central Executive Committee of the Communist party. "Comrades, it is Easter," said one member as some old instinct brought the assembly to its feet. "Let us go home."

Probably the story was not true. Certainly it could not be true today, when the makers of the revolution, men with roots in the past and memories of another world, are growing fewer and fewer. The church bells rang for a while but all but a few are now silenced. Most of the 400 churches of Moscow, which used to call itself "the third Rome," are demolished or used for other purposes. The church has again an official place in the Soviet Union, but as an agency of the state; on the same terms the religious leaders being imprisoned and executed as "traitors" in the countries under Soviet control would be tolerated. When Caesar is also God there can be no divided tribute.

Yet the people of Russia have roots and memories far older than the revolution. In few countries are folkways so stubborn and traditions so strong. That is partly because Russia has always lived behind the Iron Curtain which an almost pathologically secretive ruling clique has extended wherever its writ runs. The changes that have taken place in thirty-three years are less astonishing to the curious observer than the things that have not changed. The past is nowhere so indestructible; it keeps coming back. In the books written by Soviet citizens who have fled from the U.S.S.R. what sticks out is the old Russia, struggling to survive. "Why I Escaped," for instance, the story of Peter Pirogov, born too late to be anything but a pure product of the system, depicts villages that differ from villages in Tolstoy's time only in their poorer rations and their resistance to collectivization. Their thoughts, habits, customs, amusements, the limits of their horizon, are the same.

The hardest of all deep-rooted traditions to kill is the religious tradition. Easter was the great festival in the old Russian calendar. The largest compound in Jerusalem, used in recent years as police headquarters, was built to house pilgrims who used to go in overwhelming numbers from "Holy Russia" to visit the Holy Places in Holy Week. They were, people said, "naturally" religious; where other people counted "bodies," their census counted "souls."

But the Communists substitute dialectical materialism for the natural law, which is the basis of the moral law. In that philosophy there is no place for the soul and no answer to the questions that beset men in times of darkness and confusion.

This year the setting for the Easter message is anything but bright for any of us. We live in a world in which men seem to have lost their way, the familiar landscape appears to be dissolving and the old signposts are down. Perhaps for the first time in history, we live with the thought of annihilation, afraid of the monstrous forces of destruction we have conjured out of the elements. It is not to be supposed that the Russians are any happier than we are in the spectral presence of atom and hydrogen bombs, but they have less to say about it, and in their helplessness they must turn more eagerly to their old faith in the ringing Easter promise of the victory of the spirit, of life over death.

For a large part of the world, Holy Week, the Passover season, Easter, come as reminders as regular as the spring that life does renew itself. Nature and the God of nature never yield to destruction. The waters recede, and then the springs flow again, the rivers fill—and life goes on. Crisis succeeds crisis, and life goes on. American policy is tangled up in a web of uncertain judgments, petty angers, loose talk that echoes around the globe and causes doubt and wavering among people who are only as firm as we are firm. And then common sense returns and responsible leaders in both parties close ranks and prepare to recover lost ground.

The promise of life depends on the will and the worthiness to live. There will be many Easter sermons tomorrow, all variations on the single theme that the spirit of man is immortal. But the corollary of this assurance, never so timely as now, is that men, and nations as well, have to keep the spirit alive. Life goes on, but not by itself.

38

FAITH FOR A TROUBLED
CHRISTMAS TIME

December 24, 1950

The Cathedral of Chartres is a credo in stone. For 700 years
it has towered above the gray-green plain of the Beauce as a
sign of what men can do if they believe strongly enough and
work freely together for a common end. It is very calm, this
medieval sanctuary, very sure of itself amid the fears of
France and the uncertainties of the modern world. Perhaps
this is why, on this Christmas when the dark, unbelievable
threat of war once more overshadows the earth, the mind
turns to Chartres for reassurance. To Chartres, because of all
the monuments that punctuate the continued story of Western civilization this stands out from the rest because it states
so simply a fact of supreme importance in the present crisis.
Built by the voluntary cooperation of people dedicated to a

cause, it tells us that the power of the spirit thus fired and fused, will always overcome brute force.

From the cave of Bethlehem to the Cathedral of Chartres is a long way across time and space. Yet both in their different ways tell the same story—the story of the instinctive yearning of the finite heart for contact with the infinite. The great medieval churches were built in a passion to erect altars splendid enough to lure Divinity from heaven to dwell with man upon the earth. And year after year Christmas is celebrated by the faithful and the faithless with symbols of joy—carols and candles and trees and a vast splurge of giving—because the Nativity represents this immemorial wish come true. Of all the old churches, Chartres succeeds best, perhaps, in satisfying the desire for a House that invites and suggests the presence of God.

Chartres was built in the Age of Faith, when religion was the dynamic force that set the First Crusade in motion and covered the continent of Europe with cathedrals; when people believed in God, in themselves, in life but not in death, for at no time were they so sure of their immortal destiny.

It was built when the cult of Chivalry blossomed suddenly in a rude and warlike world, and devotion to the Virgin inspired painting, poetry, architecture and that strange flowering of "courteous love" which grafted so many delicate refinements on the rough manners of the time. The subtle fancy of Henry Adams, given full rein in his rhapsodic study of Chartres, imagines that the builders strove to gratify what they supposed to be the taste of the Virgin. If so, Our Lady must have admired the Gothic, for this cathedral is only one of scores of "Notre Dames" that were erected in the period that carried Gothic art to its grand climax.

It was built by the people, literally all the people, with

their own hands. The whole countryside, nobles and peasants, priests and artisans, cut the hard stone from quarries five miles away and harnessed themselves to carts to drag it to the site. They put up the walls and arches and carved the portals, corbels and cornices in a kind of rapture of creation, each man to his own taste and humor. It was a merry work, say the contemporary chroniclers, as well as a pious one, accompanied by prayers recited in common and lusty canticles of praise.

This spirit was built into the church with the stone. The construction of Chartres was a community enterprise if ever there was one. The labor, the skill, the genius and the love of thousands of ordinary folk went into it. They must have worked to a plan; but the master architect, the sculptors, the glaziers, whose art has never since been equaled, are as anonymous as the crowd.

A well-intentioned American social worker in Coutance complained, after the late war, that the people of that badly smashed town insisted on repairing their cathedral first, when what they needed most was houses and a community center. She did not perceive that to Coutance the cathedral is the center of the community, its identification mark and the sign of its continuity. Coutance, like Chartres, was a community enterprise, and a competitive enterprise, too, for both were built when all the neighboring dioceses entered into a zealous rivalry to provide bigger and better Houses of God.

A visit to Chartres is a journey into another time, another world, another spiritual climate. If you go as a skeptic, doubting all creeds, you cannot doubt the power and reality of the faith that reared those walls—so strongly that there is not a crack in them to this day. If you go as a lover of art

to visit a museum, you end up as a worshiper in a church, for
you feel at once that the jewelers who made the rose windows
and the draftsmen who framed them in filigree were not
creating masterpieces but singing their psalms in color—
such a symphony of color!—and saying their prayers in
stone.

If, like most visitors, you are just a troubled pilgrim of
the year 1950, groping for answers to torturing questions,
you understand the meaning of the old concept of the church
as sanctuary. Chartres is sanctuary. For a little while it is a
place of refuge from the snarling voices of Lake Success and
the dooms-day tick of the atom bomb. For a little while the
fog of the twentieth century is transmuted by the thirteenth-
century glass into a clear radiance. For a little while, envel-
oped in a serenity that time and storm have not shaken, you
feel the strange, forgotten comfort of safety and repose.

This, you say, is the reality, and the scene outside is unreal.
In one sense this is true; the spiritual resources we mobilize
for the secular conflict are weapons more effective than guns.
Chartres is the survivor of an age of inner certainty. The
Middle Age knew poverty, inequality, cruelty and war. As
much as ours it was a time of transition. Despite the legends,
it was an epoch of intense traffic in ideas and an enormous
appetite for novelty. Nations were dissolving and taking
shape. It was an age of small kingdoms, duchies, fiefs, in
which patriotism, such as it was, was local rather than
national. The letters of the time, especially those from bishop
to bishop describing the building of the cathedrals, reflect a
life that was narrow, hard, primitive, dangerous, yet full of
movement, creative energy and robust confidence.

Men who believe in God believe in the triumph of good.
Because of that faith they seem happy in retrospect, no

doubt happier than they were, and a faint aroma of that happiness lingers in the Cathedral, and even the town it watches over, although there it is more a memory than a presence. Like most capitals Paris is wracked by fear, and resentments born of fear, but in the country the tension eases. On the road to Chartres it all but fades away in the picture of tranquil and careful husbandry. And when suddenly the unequal spires rise in the opaline sky that softens the French landscape and then, set above the climbing town like a strong sentinel, the calm bulk of the church, the spirit rises to meet this sign of permanence in a shaken world.

Behind the apse a little green garden looks down on the spreading plain. Perhaps the old ladies in white caps sorting greens were not as contented as they looked. The townsmen idling in the Sunday afternoon sun may not have been as cheerful as they sounded. Of course the children were genuinely merry as they chased a little brown dog around the buttresses. Even the American playing with his camera seemed to forget the crowding cares of every day. It was a happy scene; in the shadow of the Rock we all relaxed a little.

The pilgrim of 1950 cannot escape from the terrible dilemmas of the present by going back to the past. But neither can he escape from the eternal verities that are the same yesterday, today and forever. The moral bases on which life rests do not change. The difference between matter and spirit, good and evil, truth and falsehood, does not alter because we have invaded the stratosphere and smashed the atom. We cannot look farther and deeper into the heart of things through color television than through the colored glass the medieval artist used to illuminate the mysteries of religion. The overlay of progress and invention, speed and comfort, does not cover the fact that the individual conscience is the final arbiter in a free society. In the ultimate decisions man is always alone with his soul.

The fundamental realities are spiritual realities, and the crux of the Soviet battle is that it is not primarily for material things—territory or empire, riches or physical security. It is for dominion over the soul. For the first time a powerful adversary not only rejects our civilization but fights to destroy everything we value—laws, moral standards, traditions, the very pattern of our thoughts and lives.

Never was the moral issue so clear. The choice is more radical than that posed by the most violent social revolution because it goes beyond ways of living, forms of government or ownership of property—all economic, social and political isms—into the depths where the elemental rights of man are rooted and where all that makes human existence bearable, much less a great spiritual adventure, can be destroyed.

A battle between good and evil cannot be won by arms and numbers alone, thank God, or the Dragon might defeat Saint George. It can be won only if those who fight on the side of the angels have an unshakable belief in their cause and are united by that belief into an unshakable force. Chartres is worth thinking of this Christmas because it is the Christmas story told in stone. And because it has stood for seven hundred years as a sign of the power of faith.

39

AND ONCE MORE UPON
THE MIDNIGHT AIR

December 25, 1950

Peculiarly symbolic of this Christmas time is the curtain of twinkling lights suspended like a starry sky over the crowds that gather in Rockefeller Plaza to admire the gleaming tree and listen to the lilt of old carols. It is meant to bring to the heart of New York, this glittering generalization that includes everything a city ever was or will be, in dream or nightmare, a reminder of the little town of Bethlehem, no bigger now than it ever was, and little changed since that "midnight clear" when the shepherds on the encircling hills were frightened by an odd commotion in the heavens— strange music, an unknown star, the stir of wings and the trumpet voice of an angel.

The surprising thing is that the stage-set in Rockefeller

Center does serve to remind the jostling throngs on Fifth Avenue of the best-remembered and best-loved drama of all time. You can see it in their faces as they pause to look up at the electric stars. A tired mother, arms full of packages, stops to tell a dazzled little boy about the Child born in a stable and the Wise Men who followed a star to find Him. A dapper old gentleman hums a few bars of "Come, All Ye Faithful." Soon the people around him, especially an Italian toy vender with the stout remains of a tenor robusto voice, join in. The traffic on Fifth Avenue is tied up for blocks as taxis and private cars halt for a moment to see the sight.

The scene is symbolic because for this day people in this country and every other are trying to interpose a private sky, bright with stars, between Christmas and the clouded firmament that overhangs the earth. For this day they weave a curtain of remembered joys, familiar customs, friendships and family ties, to shut out the encircling gloom. Nearly everyone qualifies his Christmas greeting; yet the qualification is a kind of challenge. "Be as merry as you can," they say, and proceed to demonstrate how merry people can be in the lengthening shadow of the powers of darkness.

The world that celebrates today's feast does so in a mood of determined, almost defiant gaiety. And seldom has piety been mixed so strongly with the Yuletide spirit. It is a self-conscious and special Christmas in the sense that many who are used to observing it as a holiday, a time of friendly wishes, gifts and fun for the children, keep it this year as an act of faith in the virtues and values that will certainly be destroyed if they are not maintained and defended. When the President declared that never has a Christmas seemed so important he was echoing the thought of millions who have suddenly envisaged a world without Christmas and all it stands for.

This emotional undercurrent runs through the observance everywhere. Reports from France and England, Germany and Italy indicate that for years the observance has not been so extravagant in the worldly and so widespread in the religious sense. In Palestine, Jews and Moslems cooperated in opening the road to Bethlehem for the largest number of visitors in a decade. The Israeli Government provided special facilities for travelers to the Christian town of Nazareth. King Abdullah of Jordan sent a special guard and a band to honor the pilgrims to the midnight mass in Bethlehem. In Rome the last pilgrims of the Holy Year crowded the wide-armed basilica of St. Peter's to assist at the closing of the jubilee door and hear the Pope's appeal for peace.

Even in Russia the fir trees in the parks are crowned with red stars as a substitute for the Star of Bethlehem and bread and circuses are offered to make the people forget the joy they once took in Christmas. "That was when we were 'souls' instead of numbers in a police book," muttered an old Russian waiter on a Christmas spent in Moscow before the war.

The Soviet creed, supposed to be based on love of humanity, has turned hate into a policy and a force as powerful as the Red Army. It hates Christmas for the same reason that it was hated by Hitler, also an apostle of hate—because it is a region of love, and a terrifying reminder of moral power. The Child born in the manger was the very symbol of weakness, poverty and helplessness. Yet he grew up to challenge and conquer the Roman world with no aid but that of a dozen fishermen and the revolutionary appeal of a gospel of mercy and the equality of man under God. Among the inheritors of that revolution there is no place for fear of the reactionary gospel of communism. The world that has known freedom will never go back to slavery. It has been proved over and over again in the Christian era that the force tyrants seem to command never stands the final test of choice.

That certainly is tied up in the Christmas message. There is something else, too, that should impress Americans as they keep the feast of giving. We are a munificent people, just now beset by doubts that we have been too generous, or that our aid to other nations should be cut down or withdrawn until they show more disposition to help themselves. But this is a day to remember not only that it is more blessed to give than to receive but that it is our immense good fortune not to be obliged to be on the receiving line, practically the one people left on earth in that happy position. To stay there, moreover, we have no choice but to help others to help us. The great Christmas lesson is that the spiritual realities are also practical realities.

40

IF THE STONE WERE ONLY
ROLLED AWAY!

March 24, 1951

A dozen troubled Easters lie behind us, and no one knows how many more years will pass before the return of spring and the feast of resurrection will be unshadowed by fear and foreboding. This year the mood of Good Friday seems more appropriate to the state of the world than the mood of Easter. But the human spirit is irrepressible, and the most striking feature of the tension which is becoming the normal condition of life on this planet is the tendency to seize any excuse to snap out of it.

This week we have seen a spectacular example of this in the way in which New York turned its eyes away from nagging events outside—the Korean war, the defense program, the wrangling of the Big Four in Paris, the crisis in Iran, the spy trials, the R. F. C. hearings in Washington—to concentrate on the sensational show of local corruption staged by the Senate Crime Investigating Committee. Everything else was forgotten, from the Soviet menace to the Easter shopping, in the spellbound absorption of an entire city in this televised exposure of underworld drama spiced and served up with politics.

And although this is the most anxious spring since 1939—more anxious than in the crises of the war because then we knew where we were going and what we had to do—the somber march of world events will not dim the perennial brightness of the Easter Parade. Between the cliffs of Rockefeller Center the lilies bloom as usual. The Easter Egg tree appears full-grown in the Metropolitan. Every altar in the crowded churches, every florist's window in the crowded streets, is a parterre of color. Tomorrow every girl on Fifth Avenue will wear flowers on her shoulder or in her new hat. If the sun shines the glittering canyons of this stony-faced town will blossom like a garden in which the flowers, like the people, never stand still. If it doesn't shine, pink bunnies and yellow chicks and painted eggs and potted plants have been distributed far and wide, enough to fill the five boroughs with the glow of spring.

It is a premature and lavish Easter, perhaps more lavish because of the universal impulse to seek distraction from chronic uncertainty. It is a customary feast snatched out of the unaccustomed currents swirling around us, a feast stressing the comforting belief that life triumphs over death. From pagan days through all the sequences of the human story all religions have celebrated this festival of renewal. The earth coming out of its deep freeze is an immemorial symbol of life emerging again from the grave.

Everywhere today people are catching at such symbols. True, they want to be distracted from questions impossible to answer because, like the sun in eclipse, only one side of the picture is visible. The crime investigation was a distraction, but one reason for the avid interest in it was that it dealt with problems the audience can understand and are able to solve by their own power if they so decide. We do not feel helpless in facing this evil as we do in beating against the mysterious walls of the Kremlin and trying to guess what goes on inside.

But people want to be reassured, too. They are groping for props to bolster their faith that the human spirit is invincible and good overcomes evil. There have been many religious wars in history, of Christians and Mohammedans, Catholics and Protestants, sect against sect, but never one in which the issue was between a fanatic nonbelief and any form of belief in God or in the inalienable rights of the individual which stems from belief in God.

So, although the Easter bonnets, the Easter eggs and the Easter parade in general represent a desire to hang on to familiar customs and gather flowers while we may, the paraders, even those who don't go to church, are buoyed up by the significance of the feast of Easter itself.

The pathetic side of all this is that human beings all over the world are aching for tranquillity, for a little time to enjoy the promise of the spring and a chance to sing "Alleluia" with thankful and untroubled hearts. More, they are aching to resume the exciting business of living and building and planning for the future. As soon as the nations of Europe began to recover from the war they began to envision a new world. Every continent is seething with thwarted movements to get going on a new track. No observer of the human scene can doubt that if the road ahead were clear we should be in the first stage of a great renaissance of creative energy, perhaps the greatest in history.

But the road is not clear. It is blocked by fear of war, and this blockade is a crime against humanity for which the Soviet leaders bear the blame. It is sometimes said that their aggressiveness is the product of their own fear. They cannot cooperate because they believe the Western World is their enemy, preparing for the attack. The answer to that is a simple question. Whom do nations mean when they ask: Will they move, or when will they move? Nobody is afraid of assault from any other quarter. Nobody in his right mind dreams of attacking Russia. What an Easter this could be, a true resurrection of spirit, if the stone that holds the world down were only rolled away!

41

ON KNOWING WHAT
TO SAY TO OURSELVES

March 31, 1951

In his speech in the Senate calling for a moral revival in government, Senator William J. Fulbright remarked that the question he raised is not just an internal domestic matter. "Without confidence in their government the people will not make the sacrifices necessary to oppose Russia successfully," he said, and went on to quote the well-known conclusion of Professor Arnold Toynbee that great civilizations have been destroyed not as a result of external aggression but as a consequence of inner corruption.

Both dicta are valid. Few happenings anywhere today are of merely local interest. The reaction to the suppression of *La Prensa*, for instance, is caused by its significance as a symptom of a disease that has proved deadly dangerous in

Europe. Even when it is not contagious, is "not an article for export," as dictators always claim at the beginning, the growth of totalitarianism in one state undermining its relations with its neighbors?

If this is true of an event in a country like Argentina, how much truer it is of occurrences in the United States, the leader and to a great extent the pattern-maker of the Western world. Everything we do is a foreign affair, including the findings of the Fulbright and Kefauver committees.

In this crisis of human society—basically a choice between codes of law and conduct—confidence in the integrity of the United States and the moral standards of its Government counts more than its physical strength or material wealth.

This is not so important as the second point: What happens to us if we lose confidence in our own Government? Some of our critics abroad seize upon the revelation of bribery and corruption as confirmation of the Marxian doctrine that "capitalist democracy" dies of inner decay. Reports from the Indian Congress of Cultural Freedom at Bombay, called for the express purpose of asserting the democratic point of view against Communist tendencies in Asia, give disturbing evidence of the inclination of the Indian speakers to regard Western democracy merely the lesser of two evils. This attitude is not confined to the Indians. Many European intellectuals, also devoutly anti-Communist, find excuse for the same kind of neutralism, or escapism, in the thesis that the American system represents materialism run wild, and that morally there is not much choice between this and the undeniable crimes of the Soviet system.

The recent investigations will help bolster up their arguments. But that does not matter if we ourselves do not lose faith. Neither Toynbee's historic precedents nor TV exposures of local gangsterism will convince Americans that they are following the downward path of past empires. The outside observer of this buoyant, teeming, restless land, buzzing with talk and electric motion, could call it many things, but not "decadent."

We still have confidence in ourselves and the energy to correct our mistakes. Senator Fulbright charges that we have lost the conscience to be shocked at corruption in government. Public scandals are not new phenomena in the United States; what is new, he says, is the "moral blindness or callousness which allows those in responsible positions to accept the practices which the facts reveal." As a means of reestablishing a higher concept of public conduct he suggests the appointment of a commission of eminent citizens of proved character and integrity to study the problem and restate the principles which would strengthen the faith of the people in the traditional precepts of our democratic society.

Such a restatement is needed, but to create the climate of faith that would make it vital requires more than a committee drafting a code of ethics. Democracy is the one form of government based on individual responsibility and to reanimate it requires a campaign of individual education in homes and schools in moral responsibility. It requires inspired political leadership to light the spark.

This country is now engaged in an extensive and expansive campaign to educate the rest of the world in the virtues and values of our form of democracy. The results are not brilliant, partly because, as James Reston* observed the other

---

* James Reston, Chief, Washington Bureau, New York Times.

day, the 8,000 persons working at this task "are primarily concerned not with the substance of what is said but with how to transmit what is said."

More than that, we don't know what to say to ourselves, and what we say abroad, important as it is, is not so fundamental as what we say at home. Capitalism in the United States, for instance, is as different from the concept and practice of capitalism elsewhere as the Soviet system at home is different from the picture Moscow and its zealous agents circulate abroad. But nobody knows the difference; in a half century of revolutionary progress we have never been able to exhibit the American capitalist system as it is to the curious world.

It is hardly too much to say that we are the loud people nobody hears and the ubiquitous people nobody knows. The moral is that what we say to ourselves and what we do here echoes more effectively on the air waves than the most eloquent message prepared for other people. The Voice of America, in short, can broadcast convincingly only the chorus that rises out of the courts, the halls of Congress, the schools, the factories, the homes and the heart of America.

42

ETERNAL MIRACLE
OF EASTER AND THE SPRING

April 12, 1952

Another Easter is another reminder that men live by hope. It is a reminder of the continuing inner life, the indestructible memories, the dauntless faith in the future that underlie and overtop passing events and external crises. These form the bedrock and the skyline, so to speak, of human existence, and they emerge into view on the age-old feasts when people turn away from the transitory turmoil in which they live to look at things that are the same yesterday, today and forever.

Year after year at this season people of every race and creed fill church and synagogue, temple and mosque, to keep faith with their past and profess belief in the future. Those who do not go to church feel dim intimations of immortality in the eternal miracle of the spring. In the free world men

almost have to hold that good overcomes evil and life con-
quers death; otherwise they could not go on fighting the
battle of today. In the captive world, too, the captives have
to hope, have to believe in resurrection, or they could not go
on waiting and enduring.

This Easter there is little to relieve the tension and
anxiety that has gripped the world so long that the human
race has almost forgotten how it feels to be at peace.
Wherever we turn the telescope there is trouble. In Korea
and Indo-China the struggle is in a new phase but no nearer
an end than it seemed last spring. Tumult has broken out in
North Africa and South Africa, Egypt, Iran, Malaya. The first
signs of political stability in France are countered by the
first omens of reaction against the new Government in
Britain. The struggle over Germany is entering another and
more dangerous stage. This country is self-absorbed and
restless.

Uncertain as the outlook is, however, he would be blind
and deaf who did not perceive a lift of spirit in the Western
community compared to last spring. At Easter time there is
always a hint of peril in the air. It ushers in the open season
for aggressive adventure. But this year the fear of fresh
aggression is diminished, certainly in Europe and to a great
extent in this country. Rightly or wrongly, the Western
Governments interpret Russia's current diplomatic offensive
as a sign of a continued confidence in the Kremlin that its
immediate objectives can be won without military action.

A good deal of the bickering that goes on among the Western Powers, together with most of the criticism of American
leadership, arises from this lessened fear of war and the growing confidence that the token forces NATO has raised in its
first year of operation are a genuine token of active strength,

and that this strength is beginning to be a shield and a deterrent. This is one reason for the general preoccupation with domestic problems. In every country these problems are overwhelming, but they would not be so all-absorbing if the outside threat had not receded a little in the minds of people and Governments.

Man is a fluent hoper. He is much more likely to yield to false hopes than to the dark counsels of despair. Year after year the spring returns. It forces its way even into the crevasses in the mountain of stone and steel that covers the rock of Manhattan Island. The big magnolia tree in the Park blossoms again. The forsythia bushes have their golden moment as heralds of the verdure and the bloom to come. The midtown canyon of Rockefeller Center is paved with lilies, and in nearly every block a flower shop offers the passerby the bright illusion that gardens grow in a city that loves flowers so extravagantly.

Whatever happens, the earth will continue to renew itself and mankind will find reasons for living in the "constants" that survive wars, Governments, revolutions and all historic changes. In Russia the biggest broom ever wielded has not swept away the religious tradition, the social customs or the character of the people. Everywhere the things that last are more astonishing than the things that pass; they last because they are part of the spirit and nature of man, proofs of the divinity that shapes our ends, and also because they are kept alive by man's faith in himself and his hope of carrying on into the future.

It happens that today the United States is the creator of such gleams of hope as exist in the secular world. This country has assumed many and sidestepped some of the obligations forced on it by its superior power. But our main mission is to keep hope alive in the community we have to lead. Confidence in the future, belief in renaissance and resurrection, is more powerful than dollars or armies in maintaining the spirit of men and the strength of nations. The point to remember at Easter is that nations have souls, too.

43

REFLECTIONS ON
THE DAY AFTER CHRISTMAS

December 26, 1953

The Christmas story never ceases to be astonishing. It is not merely that the human family does not tire of being told of the Child of Bethlehem, or that year after year wide-eyed children listen for the first time to the tale of the Infant born in a manger, surrounded by the quiet beasts, the wondering shepherds, the angels singing Hallelujahs, and finally by kings bearing gifts from the East and guided by a star. Just as a story, it is one of the most touching and wonderful in the annals of mankind.

But it is the story of a historic event, and in the context of history what came forth from that dark cave in an obscure Judean town seems constantly more amazing. For the Infant born on the first Christmas Day grew up to change the thinking and the conduct of the world. Mary and Joseph went to Bethlehem from Nazareth to be enrolled in the City of David, then part of the far-flung Roman Empire. That empire crumbled when its gods fell, and the pagan gods toppled before the blast of a strange new doctrine proclaiming one God and exalting the unknown virtues of meekness and mercy.

From the Judaeo-Christian concept, preached by a handful of poor fishermen, disciples of the Son of David, came most of the great tradition of Western civilization, came the seeds of the systems of law and justice—assertions of the equality and dignity of man—that flowered in democratic government. Truly an awesome story of the illimitable power of faith.

On Thursday twenty-two American boys said good-by to all that when they walked back to the Communist ranks at Panmunjom. These misguided G. I.'s were only a small fraction of the repatriated, and there was a certain poignant appropriateness in the fact that they turned their backs on their own country and their own tradition on Christmas Eve. For what they really did was to turn their backs on Christmas and all it stands for.

In spite of its high-sounding manifestos, communism is essentially a reversion to pagan ideas. The deserting Americans were going back in time as well as direction. The irony of their choice was that they exercised it by grace of the fight made in their name by the United States and other democratic nations. And that fight for the rights of man had its genesis in the gospel of the Nazarene.

Their action injects a melancholy note into the Christmas rejoicing, but otherwise the picture is brighter than it was last year. Reports from London say that this was the best

Christmas since the war. The French scraped the barrel and came up at last with a President, to the outer world unknown and apparently colorless, but perhaps all the better in that he has no record to live down and no party position to maintain. Premier Pella's rather conglomerate party has pledged itself to stand behind him. Germany is awaiting action on the part of the occupying Powers, excited by the thought that decision of some sort is now in the cards. The Far East is tense but quiet. During this holiday season one has the impression that the problems of the world are in a moment of suspense, and people and Governments are holding their breath lest a false move or an impatient gesture disturb the trembling balance.

To some extent the world in general is released this Christmas from its immediate fears. People are gayer as they parade the lighted thoroughfares, maybe too much relaxed. But there is no doubt that the shadow that has hung over us all for so long that it creates the atmosphere of life in every land is a little lightened. In an odd way it is lightened since President Eisenhower dragged the atom bomb out into the open and proposed to confer with other leaders about its dangers and its possibilities.

Anyone who has interviewed people in other countries during the dark year that is passing knows that they are literally frightened to death by this awful specter. As much as anything it is responsible for the wave of fatalism that has threatened to defeat all our defense plans.

"Peace on earth" has been the dream of men since the angelic chorus proclaimed the meaning of the mystery of the Nativity. This year the faint, faint gleam of hope on the far horizon suggests that maybe—maybe!—the end of the war is in sight.

This explains the frantic appeals for European unity. The warnings of Secretary Dulles and the President of France can be understood only as the voice of desperation. In this Christmas message Pope Pius XII took the unusual step of intervening in the political field by begging Europe not to miss the opportunity of forming "a continental union of peoples." "If anyone asks in advance for a guarantee of success," said His Holiness, "the answer is that there is a risk, but a necessary one. The supreme incitement to action is the gravity of the moment through which Europe is struggling."

In retrospect it is tragic that "Europe"—the supranational political authority—was not created before the European Army plan was broached. Then the defense force would have been merely incidental to the larger scheme. But all this travail proves that it is hard to resist the force of reason, the trend of history. One way or another the idea of unity, even the dream of peace, must come to pass if life on earth is to survive. With the spell of Bethlehem upon us, who can doubt the force of an idea or the final victory of faith?

44

EASTER THOUGHTS
IN THE ATOMIC AGE

April 17, 1954

It's Easter again—in some ways the most troubled Easter since the war ended. Last year, in the upsurge of hope that always comes with the return of spring and the feast of Resurrection, many political wise men thought a "new phase" of East-West relationships might be beginning. Since then we have heard a great deal about "reappraisals," "new looks," "fresh approaches," and these terms undoubtedly represent a genuine effort in the anxious chancelleries of the world to try different tactics and break new ground.

Certainly two changes of some significance have occurred since last spring. It is accepted as a fact that imminent global war is not probable, and the effect of this concensus is to render the present form of conflict more crucial; Governments are digging in for a siege that is sure to be long and may be decisive. Also East and West have resumed speaking relations, and while these conferences may be no more than propaganda contests, the shift back to verbal battles likewise suggests a choice of weapons.

But when it comes down to actual policy, the "new look" does not reveal much alteration in the basic situation. How often we have watched for a "new phase" only to find Soviet policy exactly where it was.

When objectives remain the same—in one case to extend the Communist empire, in the other to preserve the free world—policy cannot change. But it can be modified, slowed down, even defeated in time, by different methods. This is what gives a truly incalculable weight to a new factor that has suddenly been thrown into the world scale.

To refer to the hydrogen bomb as a new or sudden development is as absurd as to speak of the scruples of the scientists who split the atom as "disloyal." For nine years nuclear weapons have existed. They have been used. They have been implacably and inevitably developed until they hang over the earth with a threat of unimaginable destruction. Yet not until the last two months have people begun to realize what a war of atomic weapons would mean.

It is hardly too much to say that this realization marks the difference in the mood of this Easter and last. Wherever one looks, not excluding our own country, the Easter picture is blurred by clouds of fear and suspicion, by the vapors of disputes that the voice of courageous leadership could blow away.

The hydrogen bomb looms above all these local phenomena, almost like a monstrous Easter egg overshadowing the joyous pageant of the spring. Nature and religion have combined to make a great festival of Easter. In the churches, in the flowering parks, in the florists' windows, on the excuses for hats that bob along the avenues are the flourish and pride of life. Christmas is the day of the Word made Flesh, but Easter is the day of the triumph of the spirit. In recent years it has been necessary to emphasize the message of Easter—proof for the believer of his immortal destiny, evidence for the unbeliever of nature's constant renewal of life—because mankind has lived so long with war and death, cruelty and despair.

This Easter the sudden terror of man at the instruments of destruction he has created in some strange way focuses his thought on the beauty of the spring, on the bounty of the earth itself, on the wonders of creation—and on the horrors of the kind of war that can wipe out all these glories, and the race itself, literally at one fell swoop.

The people of the world are in two embattled camps, but if in both they are as exercised about the bomb as they seem to be in the current prints, it may be that science has at last found the weapon that future wars must be fought with and that no nation can long fight against. It's an exciting thought for Easter, anyway—that Death can never conquer!

45

AN ATMOSPHERE OF HOPE*

April 19, 1954

The stranger in New York is struck by the lavishness of the Easter celebration. He is struck by the uncanny power of the spring to transform the most urban landscape in the world. Nowhere is Nature pushed into the background as in this stony, overbuilt city.

The taxi driver is the perennial poet of the metropolitan scene. "Take a good look at that," he said, slowing down at Central Park's famous magnolia. "In ten years you'll have to go to an antique shop to see a tree." But it is because trees are few that they are precious to New Yorkers. To see their blossoming branches spread over the rocky bed of the Park, to come upon a row of determined saplings budding on

* Mrs. McCormick died May 29, 1954. This was the last column she wrote.

a grimy street, to find a garden in full bloom in a crevice between tall buildings, as in Rockefeller Center, is to appreciate wonders the dwellers in garden cities take for granted.

But it takes a stranger to observe how fantastic the pattern is. In Manhattan's new towers glass is more conspicuous than steel and concrete, with the result that the sunlight sparkles on the crystal walls with a strange glitter, a little as if they were pinnacles of ice. "You are becoming a transparent city, in which everything is reflected," said the stranger.

What impressed him most of all on the New York scene was the smiling faces of the people. And in truth the Easter parade was marked by an unexpected air of gaiety. The bright morning brought out the new outfits, the white hats, costumes of vivid color, flowers galore, and the crowds that streamed out of the churches, strolled in the Park, promenaded up and down the avenues, were cheerful crowds, in tune with the alleluias, radiant as the spring flowers that banked the altars. "How young and carefree you are," mused the stranger. "You do not reflect our sadness."

But as a matter of fact, more people are aware in this country than in any other that the next three or four months hold possibilities of great danger. The alarmist utterances these days come from the United States rather than from Europe or Asia. The American public has heard statements from the Secretary of State, and now the Vice President, that sound like warnings that the war in Indo-China is touch and go and that the United States may be called upon to intervene.

In spite of this dark uncertainty, perhaps because of it, it is heartening to read that everywhere Easter was celebrated with unusual fervor. In Rome Pope Pius XII, in his first major broadcast since his illness, made a moving appeal for an international ban on using atom and hydrogen bombs except in self-defense. This address was on the eve of another attempt by the United Nations, which meets today in New York, to clear the decks for a consideration of President Eisenhower's proposal for an international pool of atomic energy.

In Jerusalem, the tense atmosphere of the divided city did not prevent the usual Resurrection services in the Church of the Holy Sepulcher. The King of Jordan broadcast an appeal for peace that could be—though it probably isn't—a prelude to the decision of the Arab States to sit down with the Israeli in a real effort to find a formula of peace for that seething region.

In Germany a new bell named for Chancellor Adenauer was hung in the church of the village where he lives. Ireland launched a great "homecoming" festival for the Irish all over the world. Even Moscow announced a greater supply of chocolates and sweets for the Russian Easter, once the greatest holiday of the year. And so it goes—a reminder that Easter flourishes as a sign that mankind will never relinquish hope.